I0426703

# TURNING CHAOS
# INTO GOLD

THE ALCHEMY OF WOMEN'S LEADERSHIP

THE GROWTH LEADER COLLECTION

## KIMBERLY BURK CORDOVA

# COPYRIGHT

Copyright © 2026 Thrive Collective

All rights reserved.

No part of this publication may be reproduced, stored in a retrieval system, or transmitted in any form or by any means, electronic, mechanical, photocopying, recording, scanning, or otherwise, without the prior written permission of the publisher, except as permitted by applicable copyright law.

For permissions, contact the publisher via https://www.ThriveCollectiveHQ.com

This publication is provided for informational and educational purposes only. While the author and publisher have made every effort to ensure the accuracy of the content, they make no representations or warranties regarding completeness, reliability, or suitability. The author and publisher shall not be liable for any losses, damages, or adverse outcomes arising from the use of this material.

Any URLs or external websites referenced are provided for convenience. The author and publisher are not responsible for the content, availability, or accuracy of external sites, and links may change over time.

All trademarks, service marks, trade names, and product names referenced in this publication are the property of their respective owners. Use of these names does not imply endorsement. The author and publisher are not affiliated with, sponsored by, or endorsed by any third-party companies mentioned.

The author asserts the moral right to be identified as the author of this work.

# TABLE OF CONTENTS

# INTRODUCTION

Ah, the joys of leadership! One minute, you're feeling as powerful as Beyoncé on stage, and the next, you're pretty sure a herd of wild raccoons could run your department more efficiently. Well, buckle up, because this rollercoaster of women's leadership is full of twists, turns, and moments that will keep you hooked from start to finish.

Have you ever noticed how chaos follows us around like a lost puppy? It just adores us. For example, juggling meetings, family, and unexpected crises all at once. Embracing chaos can unlock creativity, resilience, and innovative problem-solving, key qualities for women in leadership roles. So, let's learn to laugh in the face of turmoil because if we don't, we may end up crying into our keyboards, and trust me, tears and technology don't mix.

Let's talk about challenges before you start thinking I've lost my marbles. Those pesky little gremlins seem to pop up just when we've managed to get our ducks in a row. But here's the thing about challenges: they're opportunities in disguise, waiting to teach us resilience and spark innovation. Recognizing this can fill you with hope and motivate you to see growth in every obstacle.

And change, my dear reader, is what we're all about. We're not just here to survive the storm but to dance in it. The transformation we're setting the stage for isn't just a change in our leadership style, oh no. It's about cultivating resilience, adaptability, and visionary thinking-qualities that turn chaos into a catalyst for becoming transformational leaders, like butterflies emerging from cocoons or superheroes ready to soar. Embracing resilience will help you see setbacks as stepping stones to growth.

So, whether you're a seasoned CEO, a budding manager, or just intrigued by the idea of turning chaos into gold, you're in the right place. Together, we will uncover the power of women's leadership, find humor in the chaos, turn challenges into opportunities, and set the stage for a transformation that would make even the most stoic caterpillars proud because laughter and resilience go hand in hand in leadership. Remember, you're not alone on this journey-your experiences and growth matter.

I've been down the road you're on. I've been the single mom, the late-in-life bride, the crochet enthusiast seeking calm amidst the chaos. I've managed teams in every time zone, weathered the harshest of professional storms, and still found time to debate the historical accuracy of my favorite period dramas. So, trust me when I say if I can do it, so can you.

Let's dive in, shall we? After all, there's no time like the present, and I hear chaos has just put the kettle on.

# ONE

# THE MANY FACES OF LEADERSHIP

Did you know Cleopatra wasn't just a stunning queen with a penchant for dramatic eyeliner? She was also a whip-smart linguist who spoke a dozen languages, a savvy military strategist, and an influential leader. Recognizing women like Cleopatra can inspire admiration and pride in women's leadership across history.

## Women Leaders: A Historical Perspective

### The Suffragettes: Pioneers of Political Leadership

Let's take a step back from the sands of Ancient Egypt and fast-forward to the 19th-century drawing rooms of the Western world. The air is thick with tension, rebellion, and probably some petticoat-induced discomfort. Enter the suffragettes, the fearless women who demanded the right to vote. They were the punk rockers of their era - unapologetic, outspoken, and with a rebellious streak that would make any modern-day anarchist proud. These women, like Susan B. Anthony and Emmeline Pankhurst, led a charge that changed the course of history and set the stage for women in political leadership.

### Women in Power: Rulers and Queens Throughout History

The annals of history are filled with powerful women who ruled with wisdom, strength, and, let's face it, some killer wardrobes. Queen Elizabeth I navigated political turmoil and led England into a golden age, while Catherine the Great expanded Russia's borders and bolstered its power. In recent years, leaders like Angela Merkel and Jacinda Ardern have demonstrated what it means to lead with empathy, intelligence, and resolve. These women have shown that leadership isn't about gender but skill, determination, and an excellent game plan.

**The Feminist Movement: Catalysts for Change**

Fast forward to the 20th century, when the feminist movement took the world by storm more quickly than you can say "bell-bottom jeans." Women like Gloria Steinem and Betty Friedan didn't just write about equality; they lived it, breathed it, and probably knitted it into their "smash the patriarchy" sweaters. They championed equal pay, reproductive rights, and the radical notion that women are, in fact, people. Their leadership didn't just spark change; it started a wildfire that continues to burn today.

**Trailblazers: First Women in Various Professional Fields**

In every field, there are trailblazers - women who looked at the road less traveled and said, "That seems fun; I fancy a challenge." These women broke through barriers and shattered stereotypes, proving that a woman's place is wherever she darn well pleases. From Marie Curie, the first woman to win a Nobel Prize, to Valentina Tereshkova, the first woman to venture into space, to Kamala Harris, the first female Vice President of the United States, these women blazed trails for future generations.

**Modern Icons: Women Leaders Shaping the 21st Century**

Today, women leaders are everywhere; they're not just leading - they're shaping our world in profound and lasting ways. Their influence encourages us to believe in our potential and take action.

So, as we stand on the shoulders of these giants, let's remember the lessons they've taught us. That leadership is about courage, vision, and standing up for our beliefs. Most importantly, every woman has the power to lead, inspire, and change the world, just like Cleopatra, but with less eyeliner and more sensible shoes.

So, dear reader, as we flip through the pages of history and learn from these icons, remember leadership is not a destination but a journey. And the great news is, you're already on your way. Strap in, hold on, and enjoy the ride. After all, as the great Beyoncé once said, "Who runs the world? Girls."

# The Rise and Resilience of Women Leaders

## Overcoming Barriers: Stories of Resilience

Let's start by addressing the elephant in the room: Barriers. They're like the annoying neighbor who keeps parking in your spot. No matter how often you ask them to move, they keep showing up. Whether it's the pay gap, the "pink tax," or the way society insists on viewing women as "emotional" (as if having feelings is somehow a terrible thing?), Women leaders have always faced barriers thrown in their path. But here's the fun part - they keep smashing right through them.

Take Oprah Winfrey, for instance. Born into poverty and faced with discrimination and prejudice, Oprah could have easily been another statistic. Instead, she rose to become one of the most influential women in the world, reminding us that our past does not define our future.

## Shattering Glass Ceilings: Women in Top Leadership Roles

Speaking of smashing, let's talk about glass ceilings, those invisible barriers that seem to hover out of reach, taunting us with their transparency. Women leaders have been cracking, chipping, and shattering these ceilings for years.

Indra Nooyi, former CEO of PepsiCo, didn't just break the glass ceiling; she catapulted through it. Despite cultural and gender barriers, Nooyi climbed the corporate ladder to become one of the world's top female CEOs. Under her leadership, PepsiCo saw its revenue grow by more than 80%, proving that women can lead just as effectively, if not more so, than their male counterparts.

### Leading through Crisis: Women Leaders in Times of Turmoil

Now, let's chat about crisis management. No, I'm not just talking about figuring out how to fix a printer jam five minutes before a major meeting (although that's a crisis in and of itself). Women leaders have shown incredible resilience and courage in the face of actual situations.

Take New Zealand's Prime Minister Jacinda Ardern, for example. In the aftermath of a brutal terrorist attack, Ardern didn't just offer words of comfort; she took decisive action, changing gun laws within a week and showing the world what empathetic leadership looks like.

### The Power of Persistence: Women Who Refused to Give Up

Persistence, that stubborn little flame that refuses to be extinguished, no matter how fierce the wind, is a trait often seen in women leaders.

Consider J.K. Rowling, who faced numerous rejections before finally publishing her first "Harry Potter" book. Rowling's persistence led to one of the most successful book series of all time and taught a generation of readers that it's okay to be different, unique, and a little bit magical.

### The Resilience Factor: Why Women Leaders Bounce Back

Finally, let's talk about resilience, that bungee cord of the soul that allows us to bounce back, no matter how far we fall. Women leaders, from political figures like Hillary Clinton to activists like Malala

Yousafzai, have shown repeatedly that they can take a hit and keep going.

Resilience is more than just toughness; it's about adaptability, flexibility, and the ability to learn from our failures. It's about understanding that sometimes, the only way out is through. And it's this resilience, this irrepressible spirit, that enables women leaders to rise repeatedly.

So, as we navigate the twists and turns of the leadership labyrinth, let's remember these women, their stories, and the lessons they've taught us. Remember to smash through barriers, shatter glass ceilings, lead with empathy and decisiveness, persist in adversity, and bounce back with resilience. Because that, dear readers, is the true alchemy of women's leadership. And who knows? Maybe one day, our stories will inspire future women leaders to turn their chaos into gold.

## Breaking Stereotypes: Women Leaders in Unexpected Fields

### Women in Tech: Coding a New Future

Let's start with the tech world. Picture this - a bustling Silicon Valley office, the air electrified by the hum of innovation, and the coffee more potent than a double-shot espresso. Now, who do you see in the corner office? If you're picturing a Steve Jobs look-alike, you're not alone. But hang on a minute, because women are making waves, or instead coding them, in the tech industry.

Women like Sheryl Sandberg, Marissa Mayer, and Susan Wojcicki are running some of the world's biggest tech companies. They're not just managing; they're innovating, creating, and shaping the future of technology. They're showing us that there's room for women, and plenty of it, in the world of algorithms and app development.

### The Final Frontier: Women Leaders in Space Exploration

Next stop, space! I don't know about you, but when I was a kid, I was convinced that astronauts were all square-jawed, buzz-cut sporting men who looked like they'd stepped straight out of a 1960s comic book. But guess what? Women have been defying gravity and expectations in space exploration.

Take Peggy Whitson, for example. With 665 days in space, she holds the U.S. record for the most time spent in orbit. She's shown us that a woman's place is not just in the home, the boardroom, or the Senate but also amongst the stars.

## Breaking the Mold: Women Leaders in Male-Dominated Industries

But let's bring it back down to Earth for a moment and talk about industries that men have traditionally dominated. Industries like construction, mining, and finance. If you're picturing burly men in hard hats, suits, and ties, it's time for a reality check.

Women like Denise Bode, who led the American Wind Energy Association, and Mary Barra, CEO of General Motors, are surviving and thriving in these testosterone-heavy terrains. They're proving that leadership doesn't have a gender requirement and that women can excel regardless of the playing field.

## The Game Changers: Women Leaders in Sports

Speaking of playing fields, let's talk sports. From the locker room to the boardroom, women are changing the game. Leaders like Serena Williams, who dominates the court and advocates for equal pay, and Kim Ng, the first female general manager in Major League Baseball, are transforming the world of sports.

They show us that strength, agility, and leadership come in all shapes, sizes, and genders. They're redefining what it means to be a competitor, a champion, and a leader in sports.

## Women in the Arts: Leading with Creativity

Finally, let's take a moment to appreciate the women leaders in the arts. These are the women who use their creativity, their vision, and their voice to lead. Women like Ava DuVernay, the first Black woman to direct a film nominated for a Best Picture Oscar, and Chimamanda Ngozi Adichie, whose books and speeches have sparked global conversations about feminism and identity.

These women are more than just artists; they're cultural leaders. They challenge us, move us, and inspire us. They show us the power of art as a form of expression and a tool for change.

So, women leaders are breaking stereotypes and leading in unexpected fields, whether in the tech lab, the vast expanse of space, the construction site, the sporting arena, or the artist's studio. They're coding new futures, exploring new frontiers, breaking old molds, changing the game, and leading with creativity. And in doing so, they're not just reshaping their industries; they're reshaping our world.

# Leadership Styles: A Spectrum of Influence

Now, let's switch gears and take a look at the several types of leadership styles. Picture a rainbow. Each color is distinct, yet they all come together to create something beautiful. That's just like leadership styles. Each is unique, but they all have value within the spectrum of influence.

### Transformational Leadership: Inspiring Change

Let's kick things off with transformational leadership. This style is all about inspiring change and innovation. Think of a conductor leading an orchestra. They don't play every instrument, but they guide each musician to create a harmonious symphony. That's what transformational leaders do. They inspire their team to work together towards a shared vision, fostering an environment of creativity and collaboration.

Women leaders often excel at this style of leadership. They are adept at inspiring others, encouraging innovation, and creating a vision their team can rally behind. They don't merely manage; they transform.

### Servant Leadership: Putting Others First

Next up, we have servant leadership. This style emphasizes putting others' needs first. Picture a gardener tending to her plants. She waters and prunes them, ensuring they get plenty of sunlight. A servant leader does the same for their team. They are focused on nurturing their team, fostering growth, and creating an environment where their team can thrive.

Many women leaders naturally gravitate towards this style of leadership. They are often empathetic, caring, and focused on their team's well-being. They understand that a leader's role is not to stand above others but to lift them.

### Democratic Leadership: Power to the People

Democratic leadership is all about giving power to the people. Imagine a director casting a play. She listens to each actor's audition, values their input, and makes her decisions based on the collective strengths of the cast. That's what democratic leaders do. They appreciate their team's input and make decisions by consensus.

Women leaders often excel in this style of leadership. They are skilled at fostering open communication, valuing diverse perspectives, and making collaborative decisions. They understand that leadership is not a solo act but a collective effort.

### Autocratic Leadership: Taking Charge

Now, let's talk about autocratic leadership. This style is about taking charge and making decisions independently. Picture a ship captain steering her vessel through a storm. She doesn't have time to consult with every crew member; she has to make swift, decisive decisions.

That's what autocratic leaders do. They lead with authority, making decisions quickly and effectively.

While this style might seem old-school, it can be effective in certain situations, especially during a crisis. Some women leaders, particularly those in high-pressure fields, may sometimes need to adopt an autocratic style. The key is to balance it with empathy and understanding.

**Laissez-Faire Leadership: Letting Go of the Reins**

Last but not least, we have laissez-faire leadership. This style is about letting go of the reins and allowing team members to make decisions. Imagine a teacher overseeing a group project. She provides the guidelines but allows the students to plan, make decisions, and execute the project independently. That's laissez-faire leadership.

This leadership style can be effective in creative fields or with highly skilled teams. Women leaders who foster a laissez-faire environment trust their team's abilities and give them the freedom to innovate and explore.

So, there you have it - a spectrum of leadership styles, each with strengths, challenges, and opportunities. As women leaders, we can adapt and flex our leadership style to suit the situation, the team, and the task at hand. Whether we inspire change, nurture growth, value input, make decisive decisions, or let go of the reins, we do more than lead. We're influencing, we're shaping, we're making a difference.

And remember, like the colors of a rainbow, these styles aren't mutually exclusive. You can be a transformational leader one moment and a servant leader the next. You can make autocratic decisions when necessary and foster a suitable laissez-faire environment. The key is understanding these styles, adapting them to your unique leadership approach, and applying them as needed.

So go ahead, paint your leadership rainbow with the colors that resonate with you. Create your unique spectrum of influence. After all, leadership isn't about fitting into a box; it's about breaking out of it.

# Chapter Summary

"The Many Faces of Leadership" delves into the historical evolution of women in leadership, beginning with a tribute to Cleopatra and her remarkable intelligence and leadership skills. The chapter spans critical periods, including the suffragette movement, powerful queens in history, the feminist movement, trailblazers across diverse fields, and modern icons shaping the 21st century. It underlines that leadership goes beyond gender, focusing on skills, determination, and strategic planning.

"The Rise and Resilience of Women Leaders" addresses the challenges women have faced and conquered. It highlights examples of women leaders breaking glass ceilings, navigating crises with courage, displaying persistence, and embodying resilience. The chapter encourages readers to learn from these stories and to embrace lessons in resilience, adaptability, and courage.

"Breaking Stereotypes: Women Leaders in Unexpected Fields" challenges traditional gender roles by spotlighting women excelling in male-dominated fields such as space exploration, sports, and the arts. It emphasizes how women leaders reshape various sectors, shatter molds, and lead creatively.

"Leadership Styles: A Spectrum of Influence" explores diverse leadership styles, including transformational, servant, democratic, autocratic, and laissez-faire leadership. The chapter recognizes that women leaders can adapt their styles to suit different situations, tasks, and teams. It encourages readers to paint their unique leadership rainbow, stressing that leadership involves breaking out of boxes and creating a personal spectrum of influence.

# TWO

## NAVIGATING THE LEADERSHIP LABYRINTH

Picture, if you will, a labyrinth. Its towering walls loom ominously, casting long, narrow shadows that twist and turn, creating a dizzying maze of dead ends and false starts. As a leader, you stand at the entrance, peering into the dizzying abyss, wondering if you'll ever find your way out. But here's the thing about labyrinths - every twist, turn, and dead end is an opportunity to learn, grow, and find a new path forward.

The labyrinth we're about to explore is rife with invisible barriers, balancing acts, impostor syndrome, biases, and microaggressions. But fear not, dear reader, for we're not merely wandering. We're navigating this labyrinth with intention, purpose, and the gritty determination to make even the Minotaur think twice before messing with us.

## The Glass Ceiling and Beyond

### Defining the Glass Ceiling: Invisible Barriers

Have you ever tried to reach for something only to smack your head against an invisible barrier? That, my friends, is what we call the glass ceiling - an unseen yet unyielding barrier that keeps women from reaching the upper rungs of the corporate ladder, no matter how qualified or experienced they may be. It's as frustrating as a WiFi signal disappearing just as you're about to hit 'send' on an important email.

### Shattering the Glass: Women Who Broke Through

Now, about that ceiling. There's good news and bad news. The bad news is it's still there. The good news? Women have been shattering it into a million pieces. Take Mary Barra, the CEO of General Motors, for instance. She didn't just break the glass ceiling but zoomed through it in a zero-emissions electric car. And then there's Ginni Rometty, who led IBM with such tech-savvy prowess that the glass ceiling probably shattered out of sheer awe.

### The Glass Escalator: Gender Bias in Promotion

As if the glass ceiling wasn't annoying enough, let me introduce you to its sneaky cousin: The Glass Escalator. This phenomenon occurs when men in traditionally female-dominated professions, such as nursing or teaching, are promoted more quickly than their female colleagues. It's like being stuck in a traffic jam, watching a motorcyclist effortlessly weave through the congestion. Annoying, right?

### The Glass Cliff: Risky Leadership Opportunities

When you thought we were done with the glass metaphors, here comes another: The Glass Cliff. This is when women are more likely to be put into leadership roles during times of crisis or downturn, when the risk of failure is highest. It's like being handed the controls of a plane in the middle of a turbulent storm with no co-pilot in sight. Talk about a tough gig!

### Beyond the Glass Ceiling: Creating Equitable Workplaces

So, how do we move beyond these invisible barriers? How do we create workplaces where everyone, regardless of gender, has the opportunity to succeed? Well, it starts with acknowledging the problem. It won't sort itself out like that pile of laundry you've ignored. It's about implementing strategies that promote equity and inclusion, from flexible work policies to bias training. It's about creating a workplace where the only ceilings are the ones holding up the roof.

So, the next time you face a seemingly insurmountable barrier, remember that labyrinths are designed to confuse and disorient, but they are possible to navigate. With each twist, each turn, each dead end, you're learning, growing, and getting one step closer to finding your way. After all, who needs a glass ceiling when the sky's the limit?

# Balancing Act: Professional and Personal Life

### Work-Life Balance: Myth or Reality?

Picture this: You're on a tightrope, juggling flaming torches while rescuing kittens and trying to remember if you left the iron on. Welcome to the circus act that is work-life balance. It's like trying to find a unicorn in a desert. But fear not, because even unicorns can be found if you know where to look.

Work-life balance isn't about splitting your time equally between work and life. It's about finding a rhythm that allows you to do your best work without sacrificing your well-being. It's about recognizing that you are not a robot and that rest isn't a luxury; it's a necessity.

### The Second Shift: Domestic Responsibilities

After a long day of work, you punch out and head home, ready to kick back and relax. However, reality sets in as you encounter the dishes piling up, the overflowing laundry basket, and the dust bunnies under your bed forming a union. Welcome to the second shift, the domestic labor that disproportionately burdens women.

Let's talk about housework: the accumulated dishes, the never-ending laundry, and the ongoing debate about who should empty the trash. This is the "second shift," the unpaid labor that often falls to women after completing their "first shift" at work.

Navigating this second shift can feel like navigating a maze in the dark. The key is to treat domestic responsibilities like any other project. Delegate tasks, divide and conquer, and remember that every family member is part of the team. Establish a schedule, and it's perfectly fine to ask for help. After all, you're running a household, not a one-woman show. If you need a break, it's okay to let the laundry sit for another day. Balancing the second shift requires teamwork and acknowledging that everyone plays a role in maintaining a harmonious home.

### The Sandwich Generation: Caring for Children and Parents

Now, let's talk about the sandwich generation. No, we're not talking about people with a particular affinity for PB&J. Imagine yourself as a piece of cheese, lovingly sandwiched between two slices of bread. One slice represents your kids, the other your aging parents. Welcome to the sandwich generation – women sandwiched between caring for their children and aging parents.

Being part of the sandwich generation is no easy feat, akin to a circus juggling act where family commitments, work responsibilities, and personal needs are the balls in the air. However, it's not an impossible task. The key lies in effective communication, setting boundaries, and seeking support. Remember, you're not alone in this struggle; numerous resources are available to help you navigate through this challenging time.

Finding support from other family members, relying on professional caregivers, or tapping into community resources are avenues to ease the burden. Embracing challenges and seeking assistance can make the sandwich generation's journey more manageable and fulfilling.

### Self-Care Strategies: Keeping the Balance

While juggling work and family responsibilities, prioritizing self-care becomes crucial. It goes beyond the stereotypical notions of bubble baths and spa days; it's about tending to your mental, emotional, and physical well-being. Setting boundaries, learning to say no when necessary, and prioritizing your well-being are integral aspects of this process.

Whether it's attending a yoga class, indulging in a good book, or simply taking a nap when needed, self-care isn't a selfish endeavor; it's essential. The analogy of an empty cup underscores the importance of maintaining your well-being. Amid the whirlwind of life, ensuring you eat well, get sufficient sleep, and take time to relax and de-stress isn't a luxury; it's a necessity for managing the other aspects of your life effectively.

**Flexible Work Arrangements: A New Norm**

Finally, let's talk about the future of work. In today's evolving work landscape, the traditional 9-5 grind is giving way to a new norm – flexible work arrangements. The rise of remote work and the freedom to set flexible hours have transformed the workplace, moving it from a rigid office cubicle to a comfortable home office.

Flexible work arrangements go beyond the convenience of working in pajamas; they embody a fundamental shift in work culture. It's about establishing a work environment that honors your time, acknowledges your productivity, and prioritizes your overall well-being. Breaking free from traditional work structures, these arrangements empower individuals to find a balance that suits their unique needs.

As we navigate the delicate dance between work and life, it's crucial to understand that balance doesn't imply perfection. Instead, it's about discovering a rhythm that allows you to thrive in all aspects of your life. Recognizing your humanity, acknowledging your limits, and embracing the notion that it's acceptable to take breaks are essential components of this new approach to work. Much like tightrope walkers who need to descend and rest, acknowledging our need for rest is integral to sustained productivity and personal well-being.

In this era of flexible work arrangements, the traditional 9-to-5 workday is becoming obsolete. Whether you're working from the comfort of your home, setting your hours, or engaging in job-sharing with a colleague, the essence of work is no longer confined to a specific place but is defined by the tasks you accomplish. The key to success lies in striking the right balance, allowing you to manage work and family commitments without feeling the weight of dropped responsibilities. Work is no longer just a place you go; it's something you do, and with the proper balance, you can successfully navigate the demands of both work and life.

## Women Leaders and Imposter Syndrome

### Unveiling the Layers of Imposter Syndrome: The Fraught Journey of Self-Doubt

As the dim lights of the fancy party envelop the room amidst the clinking of glasses and the murmur of conversations, a silent struggle often goes unnoticed. Imagine yourself amidst the glitz and glamour, surrounded by individuals who exude confidence and effortlessly navigate life's complexities. Yet, amid this seemingly perfect scene, there's a persistent, unsettling feeling gnawing at your core; a feeling that you're merely a spectator in a world where everyone else belongs, and you're the odd one out.

This sensation, aptly termed Impostor Syndrome, encapsulates the moment when you're convinced that someone will expose your facade at any second, revealing you as an impostor who has somehow slipped into a place where you don't belong. The internal narrative whispers incessantly, "You're not good enough. You don't deserve to be here." It's the constant fear of being unmasked, laid bare for all to see, as someone who lacks the competence, intelligence, or experience to warrant a seat at the table.

But Imposter Syndrome is more than just feeling out of place; it's a complex interplay of emotions, perceptions, and self-evaluations that undermine one's sense of worth and accomplishment. It's the insidious notion that no matter how far you've come or what you've achieved, you're still just a pretender, a charlatan masquerading as a competent professional. It's like being cast in a role you never auditioned for, yet somehow finding yourself on stage, struggling to remember your lines while the audience waits expectantly for you to falter.

At its core, Imposter Syndrome is a psychological phenomenon that transcends mere insecurity; it's a profound disconnect between external validation and internal belief. Despite accolades, achievements, and recognition from others, individuals grappling with Imposter Syndrome remain plagued by self-doubt, unable to internalize their successes or acknowledge their capabilities. It's as though a shadow looms over every accomplishment, casting doubt on its legitimacy and attributing it to luck, timing, or some other external factor.

Moreover, Imposter Syndrome is not limited to a specific demographic or profession; it's a pervasive experience that can afflict anyone, regardless of their background, education, or accomplishments. From seasoned professionals to budding entrepreneurs, from high-achieving students to seasoned executives, Imposter Syndrome knows no bounds. It thrives in environments where expectations run high and standards seem unattainable, breeding feelings of inadequacy and unworthiness in its wake.

Yet, despite its prevalence and profound impact, Imposter Syndrome often remains shrouded in silence, concealed behind masks of competence and confidence. Many who grapple with these feelings suffer in silence, fearing judgment or dismissal if they were to admit their struggles. Consequently, the cycle perpetuates, with individuals trapped in a relentless pursuit of perfection, striving to prove their worthiness while battling their inner demons.

Recognizing the existence of imposter syndrome is the crucial first step in overcoming it. By acknowledging the pervasive nature of self-doubt and embracing vulnerability, individuals can dismantle the walls of insecurity and cultivate a healthier relationship with success and self-worth. Through self-reflection, peer support, and a willingness to challenge distorted beliefs, it's possible to rewrite the narrative of Impostor Syndrome, transforming it from a crippling burden into a catalyst for growth and self-discovery.

Imposter Syndrome is not merely a fleeting feeling of inadequacy; it's a multifaceted phenomenon that permeates every aspect of one's personal and professional life. It's a journey fraught with uncertainty and self-doubt, but also an opportunity for introspection and empowerment. By peeling back the layers of Imposter Syndrome, individuals can uncover the truth beneath the facade, reclaim their sense of authenticity, and embrace their inherent worthiness.

**The Confidence Gap: A Challenging Abyss of Perception**

The Confidence Gap stands as a formidable obstacle for many aspiring leaders. This vast expanse separates the reality of their capabilities from the perception of their competence. It's akin to gazing into a funhouse mirror, where reflections distort reality, leaving individuals questioning the validity of their skills and potential. In this labyrinth of self-doubt, distinguishing between genuine ability and distorted perception becomes daunting, clouding judgment and hindering progress.

For women leaders, the Confidence Gap often manifests as a gaping void that widens with each passing doubt and hesitation. Faced with societal expectations, ingrained biases, and internalized stereotypes, women frequently find themselves underestimating their abilities, downplaying their achievements, and questioning their qualifications. It's as though they're peering into a job posting, only to be met with a barrage of self-doubt that convinces them they fall short of the mark, even when they possess the requisite skills and experience.

Conversely, their male counterparts approach the same opportunities with unwavering confidence, viewing themselves as inherently qualified and deserving of success. Despite meeting only a fraction of the listed criteria, they see a job posting and exude certainty in their suitability for the role. It's a stark contrast fueled by societal norms and cultural expectations, perpetuating disparities in leadership representation and perpetuating the cycle of self-doubt among women.

### Bridging the Gap: Strategies for Empowerment and Growth

Overcoming the Confidence Gap requires a concerted effort to challenge ingrained beliefs, confront internalized biases, and cultivate a mindset of self-assurance and empowerment. It's about recognizing the inherent worth and potential within oneself, despite the voices of doubt that seek to undermine confidence and derail progress. Here are some strategies to navigate this challenging terrain:

1. **Embrace Your Achievements:** Take stock of your small or insignificant accomplishments. Celebrate your successes and acknowledge the hard work and dedication that contributed to them. Recognizing your achievements can counteract feelings of inadequacy and cultivate a sense of self-worth.
2. **Challenge Negative Self-Talk:** Become aware of the internal dialogue that fuels self-doubt and negativity. When confronted with thoughts of inadequacy or unworthiness, challenge them with evidence of your competence and past achievements. Reframe negative self-talk into positive affirmations that reinforce your capabilities and potential.
3. **Seek Support and Mentorship:** Surround yourself with a supportive network of peers, mentors, and allies who can provide guidance, encouragement, and perspective. Seek mentorship opportunities that enable you to learn from others' experiences and gain insights into navigating challenges in your leadership journey.

4. **Step Outside Your Comfort Zone:** Embrace opportunities for growth and development by stepping outside your comfort zone and taking on new challenges. Pushing yourself beyond your comfort zone can expand your skills, boost your confidence, and reaffirm your ability to thrive in diverse environments.

5. **Cultivate Resilience:** Recognize that setbacks and failures are inevitable aspects of the leadership journey. Instead of viewing them as reflections of personal inadequacy, see them as opportunities for learning and growth. Cultivate resilience in the face of adversity, drawing strength from setbacks and using them as springboards for future success.

Women leaders can bridge the Confidence Gap and unlock their full potential by implementing these strategies and adopting an initiative-taking approach to self-empowerment. It's a journey fraught with challenges and obstacles, but promises transformation and fulfillment. As we collectively strive to dismantle barriers and foster inclusive environments, let us embrace the power of confidence as a catalyst for change and a beacon of empowerment in leadership.

**Overcoming Imposter Syndrome: Strategies for Success**

To conquer Imposter Syndrome and bridge the confidence gap, one must use practical strategies that combat self-doubt and nurture self-assurance. Recognizing the impostor for what it is, a deceitful inner voice, is the first step towards reclaiming confidence and achieving success. Here are additional strategies to complement the ones mentioned:

1. **Embrace Vulnerability and Authenticity:** Instead of succumbing to perfectionist pressure, embrace vulnerability as a strength. Share your challenges and insecurities with trusted individuals who can provide support and encouragement. Authenticity fosters genuine connections and

dispels the illusion of perfection, creating space for growth and self-acceptance.

2. **Challenge Limiting Beliefs:** Identify and challenge the limiting beliefs that fuel Imposter Syndrome. When confronted with thoughts of inadequacy or unworthiness, question their validity and seek evidence to counteract them. Replace self-critical thoughts with affirmations of competence and resilience, reaffirming your capabilities and potential.

3. **Cultivate a Growth Mindset:** Embrace challenges as opportunities for learning and growth. Embrace setbacks as stepping stones towards mastery, recognizing that failure is not a reflection of personal inadequacy but a natural part of the learning process. Cultivate resilience and perseverance in adversity, leveraging setbacks as catalysts for growth and innovation.

**Celebrating Success: Owning Your Achievements**

In overcoming Imposter Syndrome, celebrating successes is a powerful antidote to self-doubt and insecurity. However, the scope of celebration extends beyond monumental achievements, encompassing everyday triumphs and milestones. Individuals can cultivate a sense of pride, confidence, and self-worth by acknowledging and embracing big and small wins. Here are additional insights to consider:

1. **Practice Gratitude:** Cultivate gratitude by reflecting on your accomplishments and expressing appreciation for the efforts that brought them to fruition. Gratitude fosters a positive mindset, shifting focus from perceived shortcomings to abundant blessings and opportunities.

2. **Share Your Successes:** Don't shy away from sharing your successes with others. Celebrate your achievements openly and authentically, inspiring those around you to recognize and celebrate their accomplishments. Sharing your journey

with others contributes to a culture of empowerment and collective upliftment.

3. **Set Meaningful Milestones:** Establish meaningful milestones that align with your personal and professional aspirations. Break down larger goals into manageable tasks and celebrate each milestone. Celebrating progress reinforces a sense of accomplishment and momentum, fueling motivation and resilience in pursuing future endeavors.

## Building Confidence: Tips for Women Leaders

Building confidence is like building a muscle. It takes time, effort, and a whole lot of persistence. But with each small victory and conquered challenge, your confidence grows slightly stronger.

Start by setting small, achievable goals. You'll gain more confidence in your abilities each time you reach a goal.

Next, surround yourself with positive influences. Find people who lift you, believe in you, and won't let you listen to that impostor voice in your head.

And finally, remember to take care of yourself. Eat well, exercise, and get plenty of rest. When you feel good physically, it's easier to feel good mentally.

So, the next time you question your abilities, doubt your achievements, or feel like a fraud, remember: You are a Leader. You are Capable. You are Deserving of Success. And no impostor, no matter how persuasive, can take that away from you.

So go ahead, walk into that fancy party. Sip that champagne. Chat with the other guests because you do belong here. You earned your place. And don't you forget it?

For women leaders navigating the complex terrain of leadership, building confidence is not just a personal endeavor but a collective journey toward empowerment and equality. Here are additional tips to bolster confidence and resilience:

1. **Cultivate Assertiveness:** Practice assertiveness in communication and decision-making, advocating for your ideas, needs, and boundaries with confidence and clarity. Assertiveness fosters respect, credibility, and influence, empowering women to assert their presence and expertise in any professional setting.
2. **Invest in Continuous Learning:** Commit to lifelong learning and skill development, seeking opportunities to expand your knowledge, expertise, and leadership capabilities. Invest in professional development initiatives, workshops, and networking opportunities that enhance your skills and broaden your perspective.
3. **Create Supportive Networks:** Build supportive networks of peers, colleagues, and allies who champion gender equality and diversity in leadership. Surround yourself with people who uplift and empower one another, fostering a sense of belonging and solidarity as you pursue common goals.

By implementing these strategies and fostering a culture of support, empowerment, and inclusion, women leaders can overcome the barriers of self-doubt and bias, paving the way for more excellent representation and impact in leadership roles. Remember, confidence is not a destination but a journey fueled by resilience, authenticity, and unwavering self-belief.

## Dealing with Bias and Microaggressions: Navigating the Minefield of Subtle Slights

### Defining Microaggressions: Subtle Slights

Imagine you're at a high-stakes meeting, ready to unveil your game-changing idea. You're riding the wave of excitement, the room pulsating with anticipation, and then...boom! Someone interjects with a comment about your appearance. It's like a record scratch, instantly halting the groove. Welcome to the world of microaggressions; those seemingly innocuous comments or actions that carry a hefty payload of bias or prejudice. Picture it as a pesky paper cut: tiny and almost negligible, but it still stings!

Microaggressions come in various forms, from offhand remarks about your gender, race, or background to subtle dismissals of your contributions or abilities. The coworker compliments your presentation by saying, "Wow, you're articulate for a woman," or the client questions your expertise based on your appearance rather than your qualifications. These seemingly minor incidents chip away at your confidence and chip into your sense of belonging, leaving you feeling marginalized and undervalued.

**Unconscious Bias: Hidden Prejudices**

Now, onto our following item: Unconscious Bias. Think of it as that sneaky little gremlin lurking in the corners of our minds, pulling the strings without us even realizing it. It's the byproduct of our brain's love for shortcuts, constantly categorizing and stereotyping to make sense of the world. But here's the kicker: just because it's unconscious doesn't mean it's harmless. Unconscious bias can influence everything from hiring decisions to workplace dynamics, erecting invisible hurdles for women leaders to navigate.

Unconscious bias can take many forms, from affinity bias (preferring people who remind us of ourselves) to confirmation bias (seeking out information confirming our beliefs). It's why resumes with traditionally male-sounding names are more likely to be selected for interviews or why women are often interrupted more frequently in meetings. It's insidious, pervasive, and deeply ingrained in our societal fabric, making it all the more challenging to root out and address.

**Responding to Microaggressions: Strategies for Success**

So, how do you tackle microaggressions head-on? Do you laugh it off, throw a witty comeback, or give them the stink eye? While there's no one-size-fits-all solution, here are a few strategies to consider.

First off, take a beat. Deep breaths. It's tempting to unleash a verbal tsunami in the heat of the moment, but a thoughtful response trumps a knee-jerk reaction. Once you've gathered your thoughts, address the situation. You don't have to go full-on warrior; a simple "Could you elaborate on that?" can nudge the perpetrator to reassess their words.

Secondly, jot it down. It might seem trivial, but if these microaggressions form a pattern, having a paper trail can be your silent superhero.

Lastly, seek backup. Contact your mentor, a trusted colleague, or your friendly HR department. You don't have to shoulder the burden alone. Having allies in your corner can provide emotional support and practical guidance as you navigate these tricky situations.

**Overcoming Bias: Creating Inclusive Workplaces**

Now, let's tackle the beast known as unconscious bias. It's a beastly battle, but one that's worth fighting. Step one: Awareness. Recognize that we're all wired with biases; it's part of the human package deal. Armed with this knowledge, it's time to challenge those assumptions. Question your gut reactions, broaden your horizons, and consciously mingle with folks who don't share your background.

In the workplace, this might mean rolling out some bias-busting training sessions, championing diversity initiatives, and ensuring that policies and procedures are as fair and inclusive as your grandma's Sunday dinners. Remember, an inclusive workplace isn't just a win for women leaders; it's a victory dance for everyone involved.

**Allyship: Supporting Others in the Face of Bias**

Last but not least, let's dive into the magic of allyship. What's an ally, you ask? The knight in shining armor wields their privilege for the greater good. The buddy throws shade when you're cut off mid-sentence, the coworker who speaks up for you when you're not in the room, and the boss who kicks discriminatory policies to the curb.

But being an ally isn't about swooping in with a cape flapping in the wind. It's about listening, learning, and leveraging your privilege to be the change-maker the world needs. It's about standing up for what's right, even when it's as comfy as a porcupine's hug. So, grab your privilege by the reins and ride into battle because every ally makes the world a little brighter for women leaders everywhere.

## Chapter Summary

So, there you have it. Bias, microaggressions, and allyship might seem like a lot to manage, but remember, you're not alone. We're all navigating this maze together, learning and finding our way one step at a time. And who knows? Maybe along the way, we'll see that the labyrinth isn't just a maze of challenges. Perhaps it's also a maze of opportunities, a chance to learn, grow, and become the leaders we were meant to be.

We can delve deeper into the labyrinth with our newly acquired knowledge and confidence muscles flexed. As we move forward, let's carry the lessons we've learned, the strength we've gained, and the resilience we've discovered. We'll need them as we explore the dazzling diversity of leadership, the power of empathy, and the influence of age and generational dynamics. So, let's take a deep breath, square our shoulders, and stride confidently into the next chapter of our leadership journey. It's going to be one heck of a ride.

In this chapter, the metaphor of a labyrinth is used to illustrate the challenges leaders, particularly women, face in their professional and personal lives. The labyrinth is depicted as a complex journey filled with invisible barriers, gender biases, and unique leadership challenges. The chapter explores the glass ceiling concept, highlighting the obstacles women face and the inspiring stories of those who have shattered it.

The discussion extends to the glass escalator and glass cliff phenomena, highlighting gender biases in promotion and the challenges of leadership roles during crises. The narrative emphasizes creating equitable workplaces and strategies to move beyond invisible barriers, including flexible work policies and bias training.

The chapter delves into the balancing act between professional and personal life, addressing the myth of work-life balance and the challenges of domestic responsibilities, particularly the "second shift" of unpaid labor. The concept of the sandwich generation is introduced, along with strategies for effective communication and support-seeking.

Self-care strategies are explored as crucial for maintaining balance amid professional and personal responsibilities. The evolving work landscape is discussed, emphasizing the shift towards flexible work arrangements, breaking free from traditional structures, and finding a balance that suits individual needs.

The chapter also examines the phenomenon of imposter syndrome, detailing its impact on leaders and strategies to overcome it. The confidence gap, particularly affecting women leaders, is discussed, along with practical tips for building confidence through small goals, positive influences, and self-care.

Bias and microaggressions are addressed, with definitions of these subtle slights and unconscious biases. Strategies for responding to microaggressions, overcoming prejudice, and creating inclusive workplaces are outlined. Allyship is introduced as a powerful tool for supporting marginalized individuals.

# THREE

# EMBRACING THE POWER OF DIVERSITY

Have you ever tried to complete a jigsaw puzzle with pieces from only one corner of the picture? Frustrating, right? That's what leadership can feel like when we neglect the power of diversity. It's like trying to paint a masterpiece with only one color. Sure, you could do it, but wouldn't it be more vibrant, nuanced, and insightful with a whole palette? Well, dear reader, prepare to dip your brush into the colorful world of intersectionality, diverse teams, and inclusive leadership, inspiring you to see the true potential of diversity.

## Intersectionality in Leadership

### Understanding the Concept of Intersectionality

Imagine you're at a bustling city intersection. Cars come from all directions, each with its destination, speed, and purpose. That's intersectionality - the complex, overlapping network of identities that make up who we are. It's recognizing that a single aspect of our identity does not define us. Still, it's the combination of our gender, race, class, sexual orientation, and other identities that shape our experiences.

Intersectionality is like a secret decoder ring, revealing the layered complexity of our identities. Coined by law professor Kimberlé Crenshaw, this term has become a critical lens through which we view and understand social inequality. It forces us to consider how different forms of discrimination can intersect and amplify each other.

**The Impact of Multiple Marginalized Identities**

Now, let's consider the impact of these intersecting identities. Think about a woman of color in a leadership role. She's not just navigating the challenges of being a woman in a male-dominated field; she's also dealing with the systemic racism ingrained in our society. It's like she's climbing a mountain with a backpack full of rocks. Each rock represents a different form of discrimination, making her journey even more challenging.

However, these challenges don't define her; they strengthen her. They equip her with unique insights, resilience, and a deep understanding of diversity. Her experiences make her a more empathetic leader, able to advocate for those facing similar challenges.

**Intersectionality and Its Influence on Leadership Styles**

Now, here's where it gets interesting. Intersectionality doesn't just shape our identity; it also influences our leadership styles. A female leader who identifies as LGBTQ+ might approach leadership differently than a woman who doesn't. She might be more attuned to issues of diversity and inclusion, more empathetic towards individuals who face discrimination, and more committed to creating an inclusive and accepting workplace.

Similarly, a woman leader with a disability might bring a unique perspective to problem-solving, innovation, and team dynamics. Her leadership style might emphasize accessibility, inclusivity, and the value of diverse perspectives.

In essence, intersectionality enriches leadership by highlighting the importance of diversity and inclusion, making leadership more effective and adaptable. It brings many experiences, perspectives, and strengths, creating a more nuanced and impactful leadership style. So, let's not shy away from exploring and embracing the intersections of our identities. Let's celebrate, learn from, and use them to paint a more vibrant picture of leadership. After all, a masterpiece comprises many different colors, not just one.

So, as we continue to navigate the labyrinth of leadership, let's appreciate the diversity of our experiences, the richness of our identities, and the strength of our unique challenges. And remember, just like a bustling city intersection, we are complex, dynamic, and constantly evolving. And that, dear reader, makes us leaders and genuinely remarkable ones.

## Building Diverse Teams: Strength in Differences

### The Value of Diverse Perspectives

Picture a potluck dinner. Each guest brings a different dish, adding a unique flavor to the spread. That's what a diverse team brings to the table - an array of perspectives, experiences, and ideas. Each team member, with their unique background and skills, contributes to the team's richness.

A diverse team is like a multi-faceted gem, each facet reflecting a different color and light. It fosters creativity, spurs innovation, and drives performance. It challenges the status quo, encourages healthy debate, and leads to better problem-solving.

In a diverse team, each member learns from the other, gaining fresh perspectives and insights. It's like traveling the world without leaving your office. You're exposed to diverse cultures, beliefs, and ways of thinking, broadening your horizons and enriching your understanding of the world.

**Strategies for Building Diverse Teams**

Now, onto the million-dollar question - how do you build a diverse team? Well, it starts with a commitment to diversity. It's about recognizing the value of diversity and making a conscious effort to foster it.

Start by widening your recruitment net. Seek out candidates from different backgrounds, cultures, and experiences. It's like planting a garden with a variety of flowers. Each flower adds a unique beauty, creating a colorful, vibrant display.

Next, ensure your hiring process is fair and unbiased. This might mean using blind hiring practices, offering flexible work arrangements, or providing unconscious bias training for your hiring managers. It's about leveling the playing field, ensuring every flower has an equal chance to bloom.

Create an inclusive culture by encouraging leaders to reflect on their biases and actively seek diverse perspectives. Implementing unconscious bias training and fostering open dialogue helps leaders recognize their own blind spots, making diversity efforts more effective and authentic.

**Overcoming Challenges in Managing Diverse Teams**

Now, let's be honest. Managing a diverse team isn't always a walk in the park. It's more like a hike up a mountain - challenging but rewarding-and it requires awareness of systemic issues like bias and inequality. Recognizing these challenges can inspire your confidence to actively participate in creating equitable workplaces.

One of the main challenges is communication. With a diverse team, there's a risk of misunderstandings or misinterpretations due to cultural differences or language barriers. It's like trying to decipher a code without a key. The solution? Foster open and transparent communication. Encourage team members to express their thoughts, ask questions, and seek clarification. It's about creating a space where everyone feels comfortable speaking their mind.

Another challenge is managing conflicts. Differences in opinion, perspectives, or working methods can sometimes lead to conflicts. But remember, conflicts aren't necessarily a bad thing. They can lead meaningful discussions, spark new ideas, and drive innovation. The key is managing conflicts effectively- listening, understanding, and finding common ground. It's like navigating a storm. It might be rough, but once you weather it, you become more assertive on the other side.

Finally, there's the challenge of unconscious bias. That sneaky voice influences our decisions and actions without realizing it. The first step to overcoming unconscious bias is to acknowledge it. The next step is to challenge it. Question your assumptions, check your biases, and consciously treat everyone fairly and equally.

Building and managing a diverse team can seem daunting. But trust me, the rewards are worth it. A diverse team is a dynamic, creative, and high-performing team. It's a team that reflects our vibrant, multi-faceted world. So, let's embrace diversity. Let's celebrate, champion, and, most importantly, harness its power. Because diversity isn't just a buzzword; it's the key to a more innovative, inclusive, and prosperous future.

# Addressing Systemic Racism: A Leadership Responsibility

### Recognizing Systemic Racism in Organizations

Picture, if you will, a weed growing in a garden. At first glance, it may seem harmless, maybe even pretty. But left unchecked, it can choke out the other plants, robbing them of vital nutrients and sunlight. Systemic racism is much like that weed. It's a deep-rooted, pervasive issue that can infiltrate organizations, creating an environment of inequality and bias.

It isn't always obvious. Sometimes, it's hidden in the subtleties of everyday operations - in recruitment practices that favor specific demographics, in promotion policies that overlook deserving employees, and in a corporate culture that subtly favors one race over others. Recognizing systemic racism requires a critical eye, a willingness to question the status quo, and the courage to face uncomfortable truths.

## The Role of Leaders in Dismantling Systemic Racism

Now, let's talk about leadership. As a leader, you're not just the captain of the ship; you're also the navigator. It's your responsibility to steer your organization away from the rocky shores of systemic racism and towards the calm waters of equality and fairness.

Dismantling systemic racism isn't a box-ticking exercise; it's a commitment to creating a fair, equitable, and inclusive workplace. It's about acknowledging systemic racism, understanding its impact, and taking active steps to combat it.

This could mean challenging your biases, educating yourself and your team about systemic racism, and listening to your employees' experiences and concerns. It could also involve advocating for policies that promote diversity and inclusion and holding yourself and others accountable for maintaining an equitable work environment.

## Implementing Policies to Combat Systemic Racism

So, how can you combat systemic racism in your organization? Well, think of it as a spring-cleaning exercise. You're not just dusting the surfaces; you're deep cleaning every nook and cranny to remove the lingering dust of systemic racism.

Start with your recruitment process. Implement fair hiring practices, such as blind resume screening and diverse interview panels. This can help eliminate bias and ensure a more diverse candidate pool.

Next, review your promotion policies. Are they based on merit, or are certain groups consistently overlooked? Implement transparent promotion criteria and consider offering mentorship programs to support and prepare employees for leadership roles.

Also, consider the importance of representation. Seeing people who look like us in positions of power can profoundly impact our sense of belonging and ambitions. Strive for diverse representation at all levels of your organization, especially in leadership roles.

Finally, foster a culture of openness and respect. Encourage employees to speak up against racism, provide diversity and inclusion training, and ensure everyone feels seen, heard, and valued.

Remember, systemic racism wasn't built in a day, and it won't be dismantled in a day, either. It's a long, ongoing process that requires commitment, courage, and consistent effort. But as leaders, we have the power to effect change, tear down the walls of systemic racism, and build in their place a foundation of equality, fairness, and respect. And that, dear reader, is a responsibility we must all take to heart.

# Strategies for Promoting Inclusive Leadership

### Cultivating a Space of Inclusion

Picture a garden. A genuinely inclusive garden has a variety of plants. Some bask in the sunlight, others thrive in the shade, some need lots of water, while others prefer drier soil. Each plant is unique and requires different conditions to flourish. The gardener's job is to ensure each plant gets what it needs to grow and thrive. That's what creating a culture of inclusion in leadership looks like. It means recognizing and valuing each team member's unique contributions and ensuring everyone has the opportunity to flourish.

Creating a culture of inclusion isn't just about having a diverse team. It's about ensuring everyone feels valued, respected, and part of the team. It's about fostering an environment where different perspectives are tolerated, actively sought out, and celebrated.

**Fostering Participation Across the Board**

Now, imagine a choir. If only the sopranos sing, the song lacks depth. But the music becomes more prosperous and complex when the altos, tenors, and basses join in. That's what encouraging participation from all team members looks like. It's not just about having everyone in the room; it's about making sure everyone's voice is heard.

Encouraging participation means allowing everyone to contribute their ideas, perspectives, and skills. It's about facilitating open dialogue, listening actively, and ensuring everyone feels comfortable speaking up.

**Encouraging Inclusive Decision-Making**

Think of a roundtable. There's no head of the table, no hierarchy. Everyone has an equal say in the discussion. This is the essence of inclusive decision-making. It's about ensuring that everyone has a seat at the table and a voice in the conversation.

Inclusive decision-making means valuing the input of all team members, not just those in leadership positions. It's about making decisions collaboratively, considering different perspectives, and ensuring they're in the best interests of the entire team.

**Providing Equal Opportunities for Growth and Development: Building a Ladder for All**

Consider, for a moment, a ladder. It stands tall, offering a pathway to ascend, a means for all to reach greater heights, not just a privileged few. Similarly, providing equal opportunities for growth and development is akin to constructing a sturdy ladder. It's about ensuring that everyone, regardless of their background or identity, has unfettered access to resources, support, and avenues for advancement.

This commitment to equal opportunities manifests in various forms within an organization. Firstly, it entails implementing comprehensive training and development programs that cater to employees' diverse needs and aspirations. Whether it's technical skills training, leadership development workshops, or mentorship initiatives, these programs empower individuals to enhance their capabilities, broaden their horizons, and seize opportunities for professional growth.

Furthermore, providing equal opportunities fosters a culture of constructive feedback and recognition. Everyone deserves fair, timely, actionable feedback that catalyzes improvement and personal development. Likewise, recognizing and rewarding performance based on merit rather than bias ensures that achievements are celebrated equitably, motivating individuals to strive for excellence and contributing to a culture of inclusivity and fairness.

In an inclusive leadership culture, every voice is valued, and individuals can lead, grow, and succeed. It's about creating an environment where diversity is celebrated, and differences are embraced as sources of strength and innovation. Just as in a vibrant garden where every plant can flourish, given the right conditions, an inclusive workplace cultivates an ecosystem where employees can thrive and contribute their unique talents and perspectives.

As we continue to navigate the complexities of leadership, let us remember that authentic leadership is not about standing above others but standing with them. It's about recognizing the inherent value in each person, amplifying their voices, and championing their growth and development. By fostering a culture of inclusion and empowerment, we create environments where everyone has the opportunity to shine and fulfill their potential.

Now, armed with a renewed understanding of the importance of diversity and inclusion in leadership, we embark on the next leg of our journey: exploring the emotional aspects of leadership. We will explore how empathy and emotional intelligence can enrich our leadership skills, cultivate stronger team relationships, and ultimately lead to more impactful and inspiring leadership. So, let's journey forward, carrying with us the lessons learned, the insights gained, and an unwavering commitment to fostering inclusive and empowering leadership at every turn. The adventure continues, and the path ahead promises to be as enlightening as it is exhilarating.

# Chapter Summary

"Embracing the Power of Diversity" explores the significance of diversity, intersectionality, and inclusive leadership. The chapter begins by likening leadership without diversity to completing a jigsaw puzzle with pieces from only one corner, emphasizing the frustration of neglecting diversity. The concept of intersectionality is introduced as a critical lens to understand the complex, overlapping network of identities that shape individuals.

The narrative delves into the impact of multiple marginalized identities, illustrating the challenges leaders with intersecting identities face. It highlights how these challenges can strengthen leaders, giving them unique insights and resilience. The chapter emphasizes that intersectionality shapes identity and influences leadership styles, enriching the leadership landscape with diverse perspectives.

Moving on to building diverse teams, the chapter likens them to a potluck dinner, where each member contributes a unique flavor. Strategies for building diverse teams are discussed, emphasizing the importance of broadening recruitment efforts, ensuring fair hiring processes, and fostering an inclusive culture. Challenges in managing diverse teams, such as communication, conflicts, and unconscious bias, are acknowledged, with suggested approaches for effective management.

The chapter then addresses systemic racism as a leadership responsibility, comparing it to a weed in a garden that can infiltrate organizations subtly. Leaders are urged to recognize and dismantle systemic racism by implementing fair recruitment and promotion policies, striving for diverse representation, and fostering a culture of openness and respect.

Strategies for promoting inclusive leadership are explored, drawing parallels to gardening and musical ensembles. The importance of cultivating a space of inclusion, encouraging participation, inclusive decision-making, and providing equal growth opportunities is emphasized. The chapter concludes by highlighting that leadership is not just about standing above others but standing with them, fostering an environment of inclusion, and recognizing the value in each unique perspective.

# FOUR

## EMOTIONS AT THE HELM
### LEADING WITH
### EMOTIONAL INTELLIGENCE

Picture yourself in a boxing ring. Your opponent is strong, quick, and unpredictable. But you're not here to fight with your fists. You're here to spar with your emotions. Welcome to the world of emotional intelligence, where empathy is your left hook, self-awareness is your right, and regulating emotions is the fancy footwork that allows you to dance amidst the chaos.

Just like a skilled boxer knows when to jab, duck, and go for a knockout punch, an emotionally intelligent leader knows when to listen, when to ask, and when to steer the team toward the common goal. But how do we get there? How do we train to become that emotionally agile leader who knows how to bob and weave through the complexities of human emotions? Roll up your sleeves, lace up your gloves, and step into the ring as we explore the world of Emotional Intelligence.

# Understanding and Leveraging Emotional Intelligence

## The Four Components of Emotional Intelligence

Emotional Intelligence is in the red corner, weighing in with four formidable components! These four components are the cornerstone of your leadership boxing repertoire, each packing a punch essential for success.

1. **Self-Awareness:** Picture yourself as a boxer meticulously studying your form. Self-awareness involves understanding your emotions, strengths, and needs, which can boost your confidence and sense of control as a leader. It's like being a detective of your psyche, always curious, always observing how your feelings influence your actions and impact those around you.

2. **Self-Regulation:** Just like a skilled boxer knows precisely when to strike and when to defend, self-regulation is about mastering the art of controlling or redirecting your emotions. It's about maintaining a steady hand on the emotional reins, refusing to let your feelings hijack your decision-making, and channeling them into balanced, controlled responses.

3. **Social Awareness:** Imagine yourself as a boxer keenly attuned to your opponent's every move. Social awareness entails understanding others' emotions and needs, helping your team feel valued and understood. It's about reading between the lines, sensing the unspoken, and connecting more deeply with those around you.

4. **Relationship Management:** And in the blue corner, delivering the knockout blow of Emotional Intelligence! Relationship management involves fostering strong connections, navigating conflicts with finesse, and orchestrating collaborative efforts toward shared goals. It's akin to a boxer working with their coach and team, each

playing their role to perfection and supporting one another in the pursuit of victory.

## The Role of Emotional Intelligence in Leadership

Just as a championship boxer relies on more than physical strength, great leaders understand that IQ and technical skills alone won't cut it in the ring of leadership. Enter Emotional Intelligence, the featherweight champion with a heavyweight impact in the leadership arena.

Emotionally intelligent leaders cultivate an environment of trust, respect, and collaboration, navigating workplace challenges with finesse and fortitude. They're like a seasoned boxer who anticipates their opponent's moves, adjusts their strategy on the fly, and maintains their composure in the face of adversity.

In a leadership context, Emotional Intelligence may manifest as a manager who recognizes signs of stress within their team and offers support or a CEO who steers their company through turbulent waters with grace and determination.

## Strategies for Enhancing Emotional Intelligence

Just as in boxing, rigorous training is essential for success. Here are some strategies to boost your Emotional Intelligence:

1. **Practice Reflection:** Dedicate time each day to reflect on your emotions and their impact on your behavior, much like a boxer reviewing their performance after a match. This ongoing self-awareness fosters growth and resilience, empowering you as a leader.
2. **Seek Feedback:** Just as a boxer relies on their coach for feedback, solicit input from your colleagues and team members to gain insights into your leadership style and its effect on others.

3. **Cultivate Empathy:** By practicing active listening, asking open-ended questions, and observing nonverbal cues, you can better anticipate team needs.

4. **Manage Stress:** Develop healthy stress-management techniques, such as meditation or regular exercise, to help you feel more resilient and maintain your emotional balance under pressure. This skill enables you to stay composed and confident during challenging moments.

Enhancing Emotional Intelligence is an ongoing journey, like preparing for a boxing match. It requires dedication, perseverance, and a willingness to learn and grow continuously. But the rewards are immense; a leadership style as resilient and effective as a world-class boxer stepping into the ring, ready to face any challenge with confidence and poise. So, keep training, refining your skills, and stepping into the leadership ring with the unwavering assurance of a true champion.

# Empathy: The Heartbeat of Inclusive Leadership

### The Importance of Empathy in Leadership

Imagine you're at a magic show. The magician pulls a rabbit out of a hat and a coin from behind your ear, and then, for his final trick, he reads your mind. That, my friend, is empathy in a nutshell. When leaders understand and share others' feelings, they build trust and deepen connections, which are vital to effective leadership.

In leadership, empathy isn't just a nice-to-have soft skill; it's an absolute necessity, a cornerstone of effective and inclusive leadership. The adhesive binds a team together during tumultuous times, unlocking a deeper understanding of its needs, motivations, and aspirations. And in the grand magic show of leadership, empathy is the mind-reading trick that leaves everyone in awe.

Empathetic leaders craft an environment where every voice is heard, every perspective valued, and every individual respected. They cultivate a sense of belonging, a culture of trust, and a spirit of collaboration. They comprehend that a team is more than just a collection of individuals working in tandem; it's a vibrant tapestry of human emotions, experiences, and relationships. And at the heart of this tapestry, weaving it all together lies empathy.

### Practicing Empathetic Listening

Let's focus on empathetic listening, the art of hearing and genuinely understanding. It's akin to being a detective, deciphering clues, piecing together the puzzle, and striving to grasp the complete picture.

Empathetic listening transcends mere hearing; it entails grasping the emotions behind those words, the unspoken sentiments, and the subtle nuances. It necessitates setting aside your preconceptions, judgments, and solutions and devoting your undivided attention to the speaker.

As a leader, empathetic listening enables you to understand your team's challenges, concerns, and ideas deeply. It empowers you to respond with empathy, respect, and assistance. It's like possessing a secret decoder ring that deciphers words into emotions and surface-level issues into profound insights.

### Encouraging Empathy in Team Interactions

Lastly, let's explore how to foster empathy within your team. Envision a conductor guiding an orchestra; each musician playing a distinct instrument, yet all listening to one another to create a harmonious symphony. That's the essence of fostering empathy in team interactions. It's about nurturing an environment where everyone listens, not just to respond but to understand.

You can instill empathy within your team by leading by example. Demonstrate empathetic listening, respond to challenges with understanding and kindness, and treat everyone with dignity and respect.

Additionally, create avenues for team members to share their experiences, ideas, and emotions. Whether through team meetings, one-on-one discussions, or team-building exercises, cultivate an environment where everyone feels comfortable expressing themselves and every voice is valued and heard.

Furthermore, champion diversity and inclusion within your team. A diverse team brings a range of experiences, perspectives, and insights. Encourage your team to embrace and learn from these differences, to seek an understanding of each other's unique journeys, and to approach every interaction with empathy and openness.

As we navigate the labyrinth of leadership, let's not overlook the power of empathy. The secret ingredient elevates a good leader to greatness and a team from functional to harmonious. So, flex your empathy muscles, hone your listening skills, and inspire your team to do the same. Remember, leadership isn't merely about guiding your team to success; it's about understanding them, connecting with them, and leading with empathy. Embrace your role as the empathetic leader your team craves; the magician who doesn't just pull a rabbit out of a hat, reads minds, and touches hearts. Because that, my friend, is the true magic of leadership.

## Navigating Difficult Conversations with Empathy: Crafting Your Playbook

### Preparing for Difficult Conversations

Imagine yourself as a soccer player gearing up for a big match. You don't just walk onto the field without a game plan, do you? Of course not. You prepare. You strategize. You anticipate the opposing team's moves. That's precisely how you should approach difficult conversations - with meticulous preparation and a well-thought-out strategy.

Begin by setting a clear objective for the conversation. What do you hope to achieve? Understanding? Resolution? Change? Establishing a clear goal can serve as your guiding beacon, steering the discussion in the right direction.

Next, endeavor to understand the other person's perspective. Put yourself in their shoes. What might they be feeling? What are their concerns? Cultivating empathy towards their viewpoint can help you approach the conversation with compassion and respect.

Finally, meticulously plan out your main points. What messages do you need to convey? What are the key points you want to articulate? Organizing your thoughts in advance can help you communicate effectively and ensure that your main messages aren't lost amidst the heat of the conversation.

**Using Empathy to Diffuse Tension**

Now, let's kick off the match. The tension is palpable, the stakes are high, and it's time for kickoff. An empathetic leader discerns how to leverage empathy to diffuse tension, like a seasoned soccer player knows when to pass, dribble, or shoot.

Commence by truly listening - not just hearing, but actively listening. Please pay attention to both the words spoken and the emotions underlying them. Are there unexpressed concerns or sentiments? Listening demonstrates respect and can serve to alleviate tension.

Next, validate their feelings. Even if you don't necessarily agree with their perspective, acknowledging their emotions can foster a sense of being heard and understood. It's akin to passing the ball back to them - it signifies that you're engaged in the dialogue.

Finally, respond with empathy. Express your comprehension of their feelings and viewpoints. Maintaining empathy can help preserve an open, respectful dialogue even during challenging conversations.

**Ensuring Fair Outcomes from Difficult Conversations**

The final whistle is nearing. The match has been arduous, but we're approaching a resolution. Like a fair soccer match concludes with a handshake, a problematic conversation should culminate in an honest and respectful resolution, irrespective of the outcome.

Initially, deliver honest feedback with tact and consideration. If criticism is necessary, frame it constructively rather than destructively. Think of it as providing feedback to a teammate - the aim is to facilitate improvement rather than demoralization.

Secondly, strive for a win-win solution. Compromise should not equate to one party prevailing at the expense of the other. Instead, endeavor to identify a resolution that respects and addresses the needs and concerns of both parties.

Finally, conclude the conversation with clear next steps. What actions need to be taken? Who is accountable for what? A well-defined action plan can ensure that the conversation yields tangible progress.

As a challenging soccer match demands skill, strategy, and empathy, so too does navigating difficult conversations. However, it's crucial to remember that the objective isn't merely to emerge victorious; it's about fostering a stronger, more cohesive team. So, lace up your boots, don your game face, and step onto the field with the unwavering confidence of a true leader. In the grand game of leadership, empathy reigns supreme as your MVP.

# Emotional Intelligence and Conflict Resolution: The Art of Culinary Diplomacy

### The Role of Emotional Intelligence in Conflict Resolution

Imagine yourself in a bustling kitchen. Pots are bubbling, timers are ticking, and chefs are bustling around with steaming trays and sharp knives. It's chaotic yet orchestrated chaos. That's precisely what conflict resolution feels like within emotional intelligence. It's about managing the heat, harmonizing flavors, and serving up a resolution that satisfies everyone's palate.

Emotional intelligence serves as the secret sauce of conflict resolution. It enables you to read the room, discern each party's concerns, and respond in a manner that de-escalates tensions. It involves tuning in to your emotions and those of others, and leveraging that awareness to navigate conversations toward a peaceful resolution.

Imagine you're the head chef; a conflict represents a complex recipe. Emotional intelligence is your taste, intuition, and gut feeling. It guides you in adding ingredients correctly at the right time. It's the difference between a bland dish and a culinary masterpiece.

### Strategies for Resolving Conflicts Effectively

Let's step into the kitchen and create a successful conflict resolution. Here are some strategies:

1. **Stay Calm and Composed:** Maintain your composure amid the chaos, like a simmering soup. Even when the heat is on, strive to remain cool-headed and composed.
2. **Listen Actively:** Truly listen to the other party's perspective rather than waiting for your turn to speak. Active listening demonstrates respect and helps you understand their viewpoint.
3. **Communicate with Clarity and Respect:** Articulate your thoughts and emotions clearly, but remember that how you communicate is as crucial as what you share. Maintain a respectful tone and considerate language.
4. **Seek Win-Win Solutions:** Aim for resolutions that benefit both parties. It's not about winning the argument but preserving relationships and fostering mutual understanding.

### Maintaining Relationships Post-Conflict

Once the dust settles and the conflict is resolved, focus on rebuilding and maintaining relationships. It's akin to tidying up after a lavish meal. Start by acknowledging the resolution and expressing appreciation for the other party's willingness to collaborate. Cultivate an environment of open communication where everyone feels empowered to express their thoughts and feelings. Remember that a single conflict does not define a relationship. Avoid harboring grudges; instead, view conflicts as opportunities to learn, strengthen bonds, and deepen understanding.

**Encouraging a Culture of Open Communication**

Finally, let's discuss prevention strategies to mitigate conflicts before they arise. Open communication serves as the linchpin. Encourage your team members to articulate their thoughts, ideas, and concerns openly. Foster an environment where everyone feels valued and heard. Transparent and open communication minimizes misunderstandings, cultivates trust, and mitigates the likelihood of conflicts. So, embrace your role as a culinary diplomat, armed with emotional intelligence, to navigate conflicts with finesse. Remember, just as a well-cooked meal is worth the heat in the kitchen, successful conflict resolution is worth the effort invested.

# Chapter Summary

In "Emotions at the Helm," readers are invited into Emotional Intelligence (EI), likened to a boxing ring where empathy, self-awareness, and emotion regulation serve as essential moves. The chapter delves into the four components of EI: self-awareness, self-regulation, social awareness, and relationship management. EI is presented as the featherweight champion in leadership, contributing to better collaboration, positive work environments, and adept crisis navigation.

Strategies for enhancing EI are outlined, emphasizing daily reflection, soliciting feedback, developing empathy, and managing stress. The narrative then shifts to empathy as the heart of inclusive leadership, stressing its importance in fostering collaboration, trust, and understanding. Empathetic listening is explored as a leadership skill, and ways to encourage team empathy are discussed.

Navigating difficult conversations with empathy is presented as a soccer match that requires preparation, understanding of perspectives, and clear communication. The section emphasizes active listening, validation of feelings, and empathetic responses. The importance of fair outcomes and clear next steps under challenging conversations parallels an appropriate soccer match ending with a handshake.

The role of EI in conflict resolution is likened to a bustling kitchen, where coordinated chaos requires emotional awareness. Strategies for effective conflict resolution involve staying calm, active listening, transparent and respectful communication, and seeking win-win solutions. The chapter concludes by highlighting the importance of maintaining relationships post-conflict and fostering a culture of open communication to prevent conflicts.

In the closing remarks, emotions are portrayed as tools and allies in leadership, promoting a productive, supportive, understanding, and emotionally intelligent workplace.

# FIVE

## AGE IS MORE THAN A NUMBER
### EMBRACING THE POWER OF GENERATIONAL DYNAMICS

Imagine strolling through a forest. As you move, you encounter trees at various stages of growth - from young saplings sprouting from the earth to mature trees standing tall and proud. Each tree, regardless of its age, contributes to the overall health and beauty of the forest. This, my dear readers, is a metaphor for the generational diversity within our workplaces. Like a forest, our teams are composed of individuals from various generations, each bringing unique strengths, perspectives, and values. Recognizing this diversity can foster appreciation and motivate leaders to value every contribution.

What if I told you that this generational diversity isn't just a fact of life but a powerful tool that can enhance your leadership skills, enrich your team dynamics, and drive performance? Astonished? Intrigued? Or are you just eager to find out more? Well, let's dig into the fertile soil of generational dynamics and uncover the roots of this fascinating aspect of leadership.

# Leading Across Generations: Challenges and Opportunities

### Understanding Generational Differences

Let's start with the basics - understanding generational differences. Picture a family reunion. The grandparents are reminiscing about rotary phones, the parents are discussing their first computers, and the kids are engrossed in their smartphones. It's not just technology that differs across generations; values, communication styles, work preferences, and motivational factors also vary.

Just as you wouldn't expect a grandparent to understand Snapchat or a teenager to appreciate a fine vinyl record, recognizing that different generations in the workplace have distinct perspectives and work styles is crucial for effective leadership.

### Motivating Multi-generational Teams

Now, imagine you're a coach for a diverse sports team. Your players range from enthusiastic rookies to seasoned veterans. Each player requires a different coaching style to bring out their best performance. The rookies might need more guidance and positive reinforcement, while the veterans might prefer autonomy and peer recognition.

Similarly, motivating a multi-generational team requires a nuanced approach. Millennials and Gen Z workers might be motivated by opportunities for growth and continuous learning, while Gen X and Baby Boomer employees might value job security and work-life balance. By understanding these generational nuances, you can tailor your motivation strategies to suit each team member, just like a skilled coach who knows how to bring out the best in each player.

### Leveraging Generational Strengths

Finally, let's talk about leveraging generational strengths. Picture a symphony orchestra. The young musicians bring fresh energy and innovative ideas, while the seasoned musicians offer wisdom and experience. Together, they create a beautiful harmony.

In the same way, each generation in the workplace brings unique strengths. Recognizing these can inspire pride and motivate leaders to foster a workplace where everyone plays their part in perfect tune.

Navigating your team's generational dynamics might seem daunting, but it's an empowering opportunity to understand, appreciate, and leverage differences. This approach can foster a sense of purpose and optimism in leadership, encouraging managers to build stronger, more collaborative teams.

## The Influence of Age on Leadership Style

### Age and Decision-Making

Imagine you're at a buffet. You have a plate in hand and an array of choices in front of you. Do you pile up on the sushi or try a bit of everything? Your decision-making process at this buffet is a lot like how we make decisions in leadership roles, and believe it or not, it has a lot to do with age.

Younger leaders, like excited buffet-goers seeing sushi for the first time, can quickly jump on new trends and innovative solutions. They may be more willing to take the plunge, experiment with new techniques, and adopt unconventional decision-making approaches. It's like piling your plate high with sushi, eager to savor the new flavors.

Conversely, seasoned leaders who've been around the block (or buffet) a few times may have a more measured approach to decision-making. They might rely more on their extensive experience, considering all options thoroughly before deciding. It's like a seasoned buffet-goer who knows the lay of the land, taking time to survey all the possibilities before carefully selecting a bit of everything.

### Age and Risk-Taking

Now, let's think back to our buffet scenario. Are you the adventurous type who goes for spicy food, knowing it might lead to heartburn later? Or do you play it safe, sticking to the familiar dishes you'll enjoy? This is a bit like how age influences risk-taking in leadership.

Younger leaders, still new to the buffet of leadership, might be more open to taking risks, trying new strategies, and challenging the status quo. They're a bit like the daring foodies, willing to risk the heartburn for the thrill of trying something new and spicy.

On the other hand, older leaders may be more cautious, having sampled many spicy dishes over the years. They usually have a higher stake in maintaining stability and might be less inclined to gamble on high-risk strategies. Like the seasoned buffet-goers who stick to their favorite dishes, older leaders often favor tried-and-true methods over unfamiliar territory.

### Age and Communication Styles

Finally, let's consider how age influences leadership communication styles. Picture yourself at a party. Do you mingle with everyone, small talk flowing effortlessly? Or do you stick to deep conversations with a few close friends? Your communication style at the party might mirror how you communicate as a leader, and that style can also be influenced by age.

Younger leaders, often more attuned to the latest social media lingo and digital communication trends, may favor a more casual, direct, and collaborative communication style. They're like the life of the party, effortlessly mingling with everyone with emoji-filled tweets and hashtags at the ready.

In contrast, older leaders, seasoned partygoers, may lean towards more formal, structured, and authoritative communication styles. They may rely more on face-to-face interactions and lengthy discussions. They're deeply engrossed in conversation, away from the noise and flash of social media.

So, as we navigate the buffet of leadership styles influenced by age, let's remember this: there's no one-size-fits-all. Whether you're a sushi lover, buffet grazer, spicy food adventurer, safe-dish selector, party mingler, or deep conversationalist, your unique approach adds value to the leadership table. So, embrace your age-influenced leadership style because whether you're a young sapling or a tall, seasoned tree, you're an essential part of the leadership forest.

# Bridging the Generational Gap in Leadership

### Cross-generational Mentoring

Picture a dance floor where an experienced tango dancer partners with a hip-hop enthusiast. With each step, they learn from each other, the tango dancer picking up the energy and innovative moves of hip-hop, and the hip-hop dancer understanding the elegance and precision of tango. Cross-generational mentoring is a dynamic interplay in which wisdom meets innovation and experience meets a fresh perspective.

Cross-generational mentoring is like a two-way street; traffic flows in both directions, and everyone benefits. The seasoned leaders share their wealth of experience, hard-earned wisdom, and valuable lessons. The younger leaders, in turn, bring fresh ideas, modern skills, and a new way of looking at things. It's a win-win situation, like a potluck dinner where everyone samples a variety of dishes.

But how do we make this dance and the traffic flow seamless? It starts with an open mind, active listening, and mutual respect. It's about understanding that every generation has something valuable to offer, that wisdom can come with age, and innovation can come with youth.

### Fostering Inter-generational Collaboration

Now, let's turn our attention to the inter-generational collaboration symphony. Imagine an orchestra where classical musicians with violins and cellos perform alongside modern pop artists with electric guitars and synthesizers. They tune into each other's rhythms, respect their unique sounds, and create a beautiful, unexpected harmony.

In the workplace, fostering intergenerational collaboration is about creating a culture of inclusion and respect, where everyone's ideas are valued, and everyone has a voice. It encourages dialogue, facilitates team-building activities, and promotes a collaborative work environment.

The key is to focus on common goals, shared values, and the strength of diversity, understanding that each generation brings unique skills, perspectives, and valuable experiences. The result is a rich tapestry of ideas, a chorus of diverse voices, and a powerhouse of skills.

**Breaking Stereotypes and Biases**

Finally, let's consider the role of stereotypes and biases. These are like outdated maps, guiding us down roads that no longer exist and leading us to dead ends. They box us into categories, define us by age, and create unnecessary barriers.

We must challenge these stereotypes and biases to bridge the generational gap in leadership. We need to stop assuming that all Baby Boomers are resistant to change or that all Millennials are job-hoppers. It's about looking beyond the label and seeing the individual.

Breaking stereotypes and biases is about promoting diversity and inclusion, educating ourselves and our teams about unconscious bias, and fostering a culture of respect and understanding. It's about creating a workplace where everyone is judged by the content of their character and the quality of their work, not the year they were born.

So, there you have it. Bridging the generational gap in leadership is like choreographing a diverse dance troupe, conducting a multi-genre orchestra, or navigating a two-way street. It's about mutual learning, collaborative harmony, and breaking free from outdated maps. It's about understanding that every generation has its dance, music, and journey. That leadership brings all these elements together in a grand performance that captivates, inspires, and leads the way forward.

With this understanding, we can now explore how age diversity enriches leadership, how we can overcome ageism, and how to create an age-inclusive culture in the workplace. As we delve deeper into the influence of age on leadership, let's continue to celebrate our differences, learn from each other, and lead with inclusivity, empathy, and respect. Because in the grand performance of leadership, every dancer, every musician, and every traveler has a part to play, and every part is crucial to the show's success.

## Embracing Age Diversity in Leadership

### Benefits of Age Diversity

Imagine walking into a library. Each book you see represents a year of life with unique stories, lessons learned, and wisdom gained. The diverse age range in your team is like this library, filled with a wealth of knowledge, experiences, and skills that span across different age groups.

Now, why is this diversity so valuable? For starters, it brings a variety of perspectives to the table. Just like a library offers a range of genres, a diverse team can provide insights, problem-solving approaches, and creative ideas.

Moreover, age diversity can foster innovation. Just as a science fiction novel can spark ideas for a historical fiction writer, the fresh perspective of a younger employee can spark new ideas in their more experienced colleagues, and vice versa.

Finally, age diversity can enhance team learning and development. In our library analogy, it's like accessing a vast collection of reference books, each offering unique knowledge and insights.

### Overcoming Ageism in Leadership

Now, let's address the elephant in the room - ageism. It's like a 'noisy library visitor,' disrupting the peaceful harmony with loud judgments and biases. Ageism can manifest in many ways, from overlooking older employees for promotion to making assumptions about a person's abilities based on their age.

To overcome ageism, we need to change our perceptions about age. Think of age as the 'library card' that gives us access to knowledge and experience. It's not a barrier but a testament to a person's journey, growth, and resilience.

Moreover, it's essential to challenge ageist stereotypes. Like not all fantasy novels are about wizards and dragons, not all young employees are tech-savvy job-hoppers, and not all older employees resist change.

**Creating an Age-Inclusive Culture**

Finally, let's explore how to create an age-inclusive culture. It's like turning our library into a welcoming space for all readers, regardless of their preferred genre or reading level.

Firstly, promote respect and value for all ages. It's about creating a culture where everyone's book, regardless of publication date, is recognized as a valuable addition to the library.

Next, provide equal opportunities for learning and development. Whether it's a newly published book or a timeless classic, every book has the potential to offer something new and enlightening.

Lastly, encourage inter-generational collaboration. Just as a book club brings together lovers of different genres, fostering cooperation across age groups can lead to richer exchanges of ideas and a more harmonious team dynamic.

So, there you have it - a journey through the 'library' of age diversity in leadership. Whether you're a newly published novella or a timeless classic, remember this - your 'story,' your 'genre,' and your 'book' play a crucial role in the 'library' of your team. So, let's embrace age diversity, challenge ageism, and create an age-inclusive culture. Because in the grand 'library' of leadership, every 'book' matters, every 'book' adds value, and every 'book' plays a part in creating a rich, diverse, and inclusive 'library'.

As we close this chapter, let's hold on to the understanding that our 'library' is ever-growing, ever-evolving, and ever-learning. It's a beautiful collection of diverse 'books,' each one contributing to the overall richness of our 'library.' Let's step forward, carrying with us the insights we've gained, the lessons we've learned, and the excitement of exploring new 'books' in the 'library' of leadership. Because as we flip the page to our next chapter, we're not just reading a book - we're creating our unique narrative in the grand 'library' of leadership. So, let's turn the page and see what the next chapter holds.

# Chapter Summary

"Age is More Than a Number: Embracing the Power of Generational Dynamics" uses the metaphor of a forest to illustrate generational diversity in the workplace. The chapter begins by highlighting the challenges and opportunities of leading across generations, emphasizing the importance of understanding generational differences, motivating multi-generational teams, and leveraging generational strengths.

The influence of age on leadership style is examined through decision-making, risk-taking, and communication styles. Younger leaders are likened to adventurous buffet-goers, while seasoned leaders are compared to those who carefully survey their options. The chapter stresses the importance of recognizing and embracing diverse leadership styles influenced by age.

"Bridging the Generational Gap in Leadership" introduces the concept of cross-generational mentoring, comparing it to a dance where wisdom and innovation meet. Fostering intergenerational collaboration is like a symphony, where different generations contribute unique skills to create a harmonious workplace. Breaking stereotypes and biases is emphasized to develop a culture of respect and understanding.

"Embracing Age Diversity in Leadership" explores the benefits of age diversity, including diverse perspectives, fostering innovation, and enhancing team learning. The chapter addresses ageism in leadership, urging a change in perceptions and challenging stereotypes. Creating an age-inclusive culture involves promoting respect, providing equal learning opportunities, and encouraging inter-generational collaboration.

The metaphor of a library symbolizes age diversity, emphasizing the value of different "books" (individuals) contributing to the overall richness of the "library" (team). The chapter concludes with a call to embrace age diversity, challenge ageism, and create an age-inclusive culture, emphasizing that every individual's unique story contributes to the grand narrative of leadership.

# SIX

## THE PHILOSOPHICAL COMPASS
### GUIDING OUR LEADERSHIP JOURNEY

"Philosophy" - the very word might evoke curiosity and a sense of relevance, reminding us that it guides our leadership choices and actions, not just academic debates.

So, please put on your thinking cap, dear reader, as we explore philosophies that can inspire your growth as a leader. From ancient Greece to modern thought, these ideas can help shape your leadership journey. Ready to reflect and grow? Let's dive in!

## The Influence of Philosophy on Leadership Styles

### Stoicism and Leadership

Imagine you're a captain sailing through a storm. The waves are high, and the wind is howling, but you remain calm, steady, and focused. This resilience is the core of Stoicism, empowering you to face challenges with confidence.

A philosophy rooted in ancient Greece, Stoicism teaches us to differentiate between what we can control and what we can't. It's about maintaining inner peace amidst external turmoil, a principle highly relevant to leaders. Just as the captain can't control the storm, leaders can't control market fluctuations, economic downturns, or office coffee machines that inexplicably break down on a Monday morning.

What leaders can control, however, is their response to these challenges. A stoic leader remains composed under pressure, makes rational decisions, and doesn't allow external circumstances to disrupt their inner equilibrium. They understand that leadership, like sailing, isn't about avoiding storms but navigating them with poise and resilience.

## Existentialism and Leadership

Now, let's shift gears from the calm waters of Stoicism to the existential questioning of Existentialism. Picture yourself standing at the edge of a cliff, looking out into the vast unknown, pondering the meaning of life, leadership, and whether you left the stove on. This introspective exploration is the crux of existentialism.

Existentialism is a philosophy that emphasizes individual existence, freedom, and choice. It's the idea that we are free agents in a random, seemingly meaningless universe, responsible for our own destiny. In a leadership context, existentialism encourages leaders to carve their own paths, make authentic decisions, and take responsibility for their actions.

An existential leader doesn't follow the crowd or stick to the script. They question, explore, and create their narrative. They understand that leadership isn't a predetermined role but a personal responsibility, an opportunity to make a unique impact.

## Feminist Philosophy and Leadership

Finally, let's turn our philosophical lens towards Feminist Philosophy, a perspective that brings us back down to earth and into social justice. Imagine you're at a rally, surrounded by passionate voices championing gender equality. This collective push toward fairness, respect, and equality is the heartbeat of feminist philosophy.

Feminist philosophy challenges traditional power structures, advocates for equality, and champions the power of the female voice. Regarding leadership, feminist philosophy is not about favoring women over men but about promoting equality, empathy, and mutual respect.

A feminist leader values diversity, practices inclusive decision-making, and advocates for equal opportunities. They lead not with authority but with empathy, collaboration, and mutual respect. They inspire not through domination but through empowerment. While applying these principles can be challenging, understanding that leadership is about lifting others as they rise helps prepare you to navigate obstacles and stay committed to your values.

So, there you have it - three influential philosophies, each offering unique insights into leadership. Whether you resonate with the serene resilience of Stoicism, the introspective freedom of Existentialism, or the empowering equality of Feminist Philosophy, remember this: Leadership is enriched by integrating diverse principles. These philosophies are not mutually exclusive but can be combined to create a nuanced, adaptable leadership style. Embrace this personal journey of continuous exploration.

## Eastern vs Western Perspectives on Leadership

### Eastern Leadership Principles

Consider a Tai Chi Master - moving with fluidity, demonstrating balance, and embodying a sense of calm control. This imagery beautifully captures the essence of Eastern leadership principles. Rooted in philosophies such as Confucianism, Taoism, and Buddhism, Eastern leadership often values harmony, humility, and collective well-being.

In the East, leaders often behave as facilitators who guide their teams gently towards set objectives, much like a river steadily flowing towards the sea. There's an emphasis on the group rather than the individual. Think of it as a tea ceremony, where every element and participant is integral to the process, contributing to the overall experience.

Respect for hierarchy is also a key element, in which leaders are seen as elder members of a family unit, deserving of respect for their wisdom and experience. However, this respect isn't a one-way street. Leaders, in turn, are expected to care for their team members, much like a gardener tending to many plants, ensuring each one thrives.

## Western Leadership Principles

Now, picture a track and field relay race. Each runner powers forward, passing the baton to the next, all eyes on the finish line. This is a fitting metaphor for Western leadership principles, which often emphasize action, results, and individual initiative.

Drawing on philosophies rooted in Greek and Roman thought, Western leadership tends towards individualistic approaches. Leaders often serve as decision-makers, driving change, setting goals, and motivating their teams to achieve these objectives. It's akin to a solo rock climber scaling a cliff, making swift decisions, taking calculated risks, and pushing forward with determination.

Additionally, Western leadership often values innovation, competitiveness, and freedom of expression. It's like a brainstorming session, where everyone is encouraged to contribute their unique ideas, challenge existing norms, and push for innovative solutions.

## Integrating Eastern and Western Approaches

Now, imagine a fusion orchestra, where Western violins blend seamlessly with Eastern sitars, creating a symphony that is both familiar and fresh. This is what integrating Eastern and Western leadership approaches can look like - a balanced blend of collective harmony and individual initiative, quiet humility and bold action, respect for hierarchy, and freedom of expression.

Incorporating Eastern principles can help leaders foster a sense of harmony and collective well-being in their teams, promoting a culture of respect and cooperation. Meanwhile, Western principles can inspire leaders to drive innovation, encourage individual initiative, and set ambitious goals.

Merging these principles is like mixing colors on a palette - creating a unique blend that offers the best of both worlds. It allows leaders to adapt their approach based on the situation, the team's needs, and the organizational culture.

Leaders who can seamlessly blend Eastern and Western principles are like bilingual speakers, fluent in the language of both leadership styles. They can easily navigate the globalized business landscape, building bridges across cultural divides and fostering an inclusive, dynamic, and effective team environment.

So, whether you lean more towards the calming Tai Chi Master or the dynamic relay racer, remember that effective leadership isn't about choosing one over the other. It's about blending different principles to create a style that is uniquely your own - much like a fusion orchestra creating a symphony that resonates with a broad audience.

Let's keep this symphony in our minds as we move forward - a reminder of the rich, diverse, and harmonious blend of leadership principles that guide us. Let's continue to explore, learn, and grow, conducting our leadership orchestra with the wisdom of the East and the innovation of the West.

# From Transactional to Transformational Leadership

### Characteristics of Transactional Leadership

Transactional leadership. It sounds like something you'd do at a bank. In many ways, it's not that far off. Picture a marketplace. You give the vendor money; they give you a bag of apples. It's a straightforward exchange that leaves both parties satisfied.

A transactional leader operates on a similar principle. They set clear goals for their team, provide the necessary resources, and expect an 'exchange' in results. It's a 'you scratch my back, I'll scratch yours' type of leadership, where rewards and corrections are doled out based on performance.

Leaders act like scorekeepers in this realm, tracking their team's performance and providing feedback based on their achievements. They're like the conductor of a well-rehearsed orchestra, guiding their musicians through a pre-determined symphony, with each note played to perfection.

Transactional leadership can be effective in achieving specific, short-term goals. It offers clear direction, provides immediate feedback, and aligns rewards with performance. But while this leadership style may hit all the right notes in some situations, it doesn't always allow for improvisation, innovation, or emotional engagement. For that, we need to change our tune and explore the realm of transformational leadership.

**Characteristics of Transformational Leadership**

Now, imagine a jazz band. There's a loose structure, but the magic happens in the improvisation, the spontaneous creation, and the emotional connection between the musicians and their audience. This is the essence of transformational leadership.

Transformational leaders don't just conduct; they inspire. They don't just set goals; they ignite a shared vision. They don't just reward results; they foster personal growth and intellectual stimulation. They're not just leaders; they're catalysts for change.

In transformational leadership, leaders are more like mentors than managers. They encourage their team to explore innovative ideas, challenge the status quo, and leave their comfort zones. These leaders don't just want their team to perform; they want them to grow, learn, and evolve.

Transformational leadership can lead to higher team satisfaction, increased productivity, and a stronger sense of team identity. It's like a jazz band in full swing, feeding off each other's energy, improvising with flair, and captivating their audience.

**Transitioning from Transactional to Transformational**

So, how do you transition from transactional to transformational leadership? It's like learning to dance. You start with the essential steps (transactional leadership), mastering the rhythm, the sequence, and the precision. But once you've got that down, you start improvising (transformational leadership) - adding a twirl here, a dip there, moving with the music and your partner in a spontaneous, creative flow.

The first step is to shift your perspective. Start seeing your team not as employees to be managed, but as individuals to be inspired. It's about moving from 'I lead, you follow' to 'We're in this together.'

Next, foster an environment of open communication and collaboration. Encourage your team to share ideas, challenge assumptions, and participate in decision-making. It's about moving from a one-way street to a bustling roundabout of ideas and feedback.

Finally, focus on your team's growth and development. Provide learning opportunities, encourage creativity, and celebrate results, effort, and innovation. It's about moving from rewarding the destination to appreciating the journey.

Remember, transitioning from transactional to transformational leadership isn't about discarding one for the other. It's about knowing when to follow the sheet music, when to improvise, when to conduct, and when to jam. It's about expanding your leadership repertoire to include a range of styles and approaches so you can lead with precision and flair, structure, and spontaneity.

# Ethical Leadership and Moral Courage

In leadership, where the principles of integrity, fairness, and honor form the bedrock, ethical leadership stands as the unwavering beacon, guiding leaders through the complexities of their roles. This chapter explores the essence of moral leadership and its role as a steady guide in turbulent times.

### Defining Ethical Leadership

Imagine a knight sworn to protect their kingdom, upholding the code of chivalry with honesty, fairness, and honor. This noble figure embodies the essence of ethical leadership. Much like our knights, ethical leaders are guided by a moral compass, leading with integrity and upholding the highest standards of conduct. In their kingdom, values are not mere posters on a wall but principles to live by. Ethical leadership is about doing what's right, standing up for justice, and setting an example for others.

### Cultivating Moral Courage

Being an ethical leader is akin to facing a fire-breathing dragon with nothing but a shield of integrity and a sword of justice. It requires moral courage – the ability to stand up for what's right in the face of resistance or personal loss. Cultivating moral courage demands self-reflection, a clear moral compass, and the willingness to act. It's about building the ethical muscle to face challenges with unwavering determination.

### Ethical Decision-Making in Leadership

Ethical decision-making is like navigating a labyrinth, where each turn represents a choice that leads to the ultimate moral outcome. It involves critical thinking, empathy, and foresight – thinking beyond immediate impacts and considering long-term consequences. Leaders must ask tough questions, explore options, and make decisions that align with ethical principles, promoting the well-being of all stakeholders.

**Role of Ethics in Crisis Management**

In the realm of leadership, crises are uninvited guests testing leadership mettle. Ethical leadership in crisis management involves navigating with integrity, making tough decisions under pressure, and prioritizing the well-being of teams and stakeholders. Whether facing a PR scandal, financial setback, or a global pandemic, an ethical leader responds with courage, integrity, and a steadfast commitment to doing what's right.

**Building Trust through Ethical Leadership**

At the heart of ethical leadership lies trust, the foundation of a castle. Ethical leaders build trust by consistently demonstrating integrity, transparency, and fairness. Trust takes time to make like a sturdy castle, but creates a strong, resilient, and loyal team. Ethical leadership is not just about following a code of conduct; it's about being a beacon of integrity, a champion of justice, and a builder of trust.

**The Steady Beacon in Turbulent Times**

Imagine yourself as a lighthouse keeper tasked with keeping the light burning no matter what. This parallels the role of ethical leaders, who provide guidance based on a solid moral compass. Ethical leaders, like dependable lighthouse keepers, stand as unwavering pillars in the vast sea of leadership. They adhere to a code of ethics, make decisions based on moral principles, and set an example for their team.

As we conclude this chapter, the symbolic journey through the vast ocean of leadership emphasizes the importance of the steady glow of ethical leadership. The guiding light of integrity, the essence of moral courage, the path of ethical decision-making, the anchor of ethics in crisis management, and the trust forged through ethical leadership collectively illuminate the way forward. In the grand tale of leadership, the voyage continues, guided by the steady beacon of moral leadership, promising new horizons, more profound exploration, and exciting challenges.

# Chapter Summary

"The Philosophical Compass: Guiding Our Leadership Journey" takes readers on a philosophical exploration of leadership, examining the influences of Stoicism, Existentialism, and Feminist Philosophy on leadership styles. The chapter invites readers to don their thinking caps and embark on a mind-expanding adventure.

Stoicism is portrayed as a philosophy that teaches composure amidst external turmoil, resonating with the calm resilience of a captain navigating through a storm. Existentialism encourages leaders to carve their own path, make authentic decisions, and take responsibility for their actions, reminiscent of standing at the edge of a cliff, pondering life's meaning. Feminist Philosophy is depicted as a collective push for gender equality, promoting inclusive, empathetic leadership that values diversity and mutual respect.

The chapter then delves into Eastern and Western perspectives on leadership. Eastern leadership principles, rooted in philosophies such as Confucianism and Taoism, emphasize harmony, humility, and collective well-being. Drawing from Greek and Roman ideologies, Western leadership leans towards individualistic approaches, emphasizing action, results, and innovation. The integration of Eastern and Western approaches is likened to a fusion orchestra, creating a balanced blend of collective harmony and individual initiative.

# SEVEN

---

# THE BOUNCE-BACK FACTOR

## CULTIVATING RESILIENCE
## IN LEADERSHIP

Picture yourself as a rubber ball. Imagine being thrown against a hard surface only to bounce back with even greater force. This, in essence, is resilience - the ability to recover quickly from difficulties, to bounce back from adversity, and to keep going despite the challenges.

Resilience, my friends, is not just for rubber balls. It's a crucial quality for leaders, a trait that enables them to weather storms, navigate challenges, and emerge stronger. Recognizing this can inspire pride and motivate current and aspiring leaders to develop resilience.

## Understanding and Cultivating Resilience

### Defining Resilience

So, what exactly is resilience? In the words of Maya Angelou, "I can be changed by what happens to me. But I refuse to be reduced by it." Resilience is this refusal to be reduced by adversity. It's the determination to rise above challenges, the ability to adapt to change, and the strength to persevere in adversity.

In leadership, resilience is about staying the course, maintaining your focus, and leading with conviction, even amid uncertainty or difficulty. A resilient leader is like a captain steering their ship through a storm, steadfast, unwavering, and undeterred by the tumultuous waves.

**The Science of Resilience**

Now, you might be wondering - what makes some people more resilient than others? Is it something in their genes, or is it a skill that can be learned? Well, it's a bit of both.

Research shows genetic makeup can influence our natural resilience, but it's not the whole story. Much like a muscle, resilience can be built and strengthened over time. Our experiences, our relationships, and our mindset shape it.

Studies suggest that resilient individuals often share optimism, a sense of purpose, and strong social connections. They also tend to view challenges as growth opportunities rather than threats. Regular self-assessment and team feedback can help gauge resilience levels and guide targeted development efforts.

**Strategies for Building Personal Resilience**

So, how can leaders at different levels tailor resilience-building practices? Much like a workout routine, it involves regular practice, various exercises, and a good dose of determination. Here are a few adaptable strategies to get you started:

1. **Cultivate a Positive Mindset**: Think of this as your warm-up exercise. Start your day with positive affirmations, practice gratitude, and maintain a hopeful outlook, even in challenging situations.
2. **Foster Strong Relationships**: This is like your team sport. Nurture your relationships, seek support when needed, and offer help to others. Remember, we're stronger together.

3. **Embrace Change**: Consider this your agility training. Learn to see change as a natural part of life and an opportunity for growth. Adapt, learn, and grow with each new challenge.
4. **Take Care of Your Health**: This is your endurance training. Regular exercise, a balanced diet, and adequate sleep can boost your physical resilience, while activities like meditation and journaling can support your mental resilience. Prioritizing self-care empowers you to face challenges with confidence.
5. **Set Realistic Goals**: This is your strength training. Having clear, achievable goals can give you a sense of purpose and direction. It's about knowing where you're heading and taking steady steps toward your destination.

Remember, building resilience is a journey, not a destination. It's about progress, not perfection. So, be patient with yourself, celebrate small victories, and keep bouncing back, no matter what. In the grand leadership game, resilience is not just about scoring a goal; it's about staying in the game, no matter how challenging the competition is.

## Leveraging Failure: Lessons from Setbacks

### Case Studies of Leaders Overcoming Failure

Imagine a phoenix rising from the ashes - a symbol of rebirth and resilience. The world of leadership is dotted with such phoenixes, leaders who have tripped, stumbled, and risen again, more robust and wiser. Let's turn the spotlight on a few of these inspiring stories.

Consider Steve Jobs, the visionary behind Apple. His trip to the valley of failure began when he was ousted from his company in 1985. Yet, he didn't let this setback define him. Instead, he founded NeXT, a computer platform development company that Apple ultimately bought. This led to his return to Apple, where he spearheaded the development of groundbreaking products like the iPod, iPhone, and iPad. Jobs' story is a powerful testament to turning failure into a stepping stone toward even greater success.

Let's also reflect on Arianna Huffington's journey. Before launching the Huffington Post, one of our time's most widely read news publications, she faced rejection after rejection. 36 publishers turned down her second book. Rather than let this discourage her, she persisted, and her continued efforts led to the creation of a media empire.

**The Role of Failure in Leadership Growth**

So, how does failure shape us as leaders? Think of it as a tough-love teacher. It challenges you and, at times, may knock you down. But it also offers valuable lessons, encouraging hope and resilience to keep moving forward.

Failure tests your mettle. It peels away the layers of comfort and complacency, laying bare your vulnerabilities. It forces you to face your weaknesses, to question your assumptions, and to rethink your strategies. It's like stumbling in the dark, only to find a switch that floods the room with light, revealing paths you hadn't noticed before.

Moreover, failure cultivates resilience. Each setback is an opportunity to practice bouncing back to develop the grit and tenacity that are hallmarks of influential leaders. It's a training ground for resilience, teaching you to take hits, dust yourself off, and keep moving forward.

**Turning Setbacks into Comebacks**

Now, how do we turn setbacks into comebacks? The answer lies in our mindset. Imagine you're a scientist, and each failure is an experiment. Instead of viewing these experiments as definitive tests of your abilities, see them as opportunities to gain experience, iterate, and improve.

Start by embracing a growth mindset. See failure not as a dead-end but as a detour leading you to a better path. View each setback as a lesson, each mistake as feedback, and each disappointment as a nudge toward a different direction.

Next, practice self-compassion. Instead of beating yourself up over a misstep, treat yourself with kindness and understanding. Remember that failure is a part of life, not a measure of your worth.

Finally, keep your eyes on the prize. Stay focused on your goals and let them pull you forward. Remember why you started, remember what you're working towards, and let that vision inspire you to rise above the setbacks.

In the grand tapestry of leadership, failures are not stains or imperfections. They're integral threads that add depth, color, and character to your leadership story. So, embrace them, learn from them, and let them guide you toward becoming a more resilient, adaptable, and effective leader.

# The Role of Self-Care
# in Resilient Leadership

### The Connection Between Self-Care and Resilience

Think of yourself as a high-performance car. To keep running smoothly, you need regular maintenance - oil changes, tire rotations, and the occasional car wash. This is self-care in a nutshell. The maintenance routine keeps your engine running smoothly, particularly when the road gets tough.

Self-care and resilience are closely intertwined, much like the engine and wheels of a car. A well-maintained engine (self-care) provides the power for the wheels to keep turning (resilience), even on rough terrain. Consistent self-care practices refuel your energy, sharpen your focus, and fortify your mental and emotional stamina.

In other words, self-care is not just about bubble baths and spa days (though those are great, too). It's about taking care of your physical, mental, and emotional health so that you can navigate leadership challenges with greater resilience.

### Practical Self-Care Strategies for Leaders

Now that we've established the importance of self-care for resilience, let's look at some practical strategies. Picture yourself in the driver's seat of your car. To keep your vehicle running smoothly, you must monitor the fuel gauge, keep the windshield clean, and have it tuned up occasionally. Here are some equivalent self-care strategies for you, the leader:

1. **Monitor Your Energy Levels**: Just as you watch your car's fuel gauge, keep an eye on your energy levels. Recognize when you're running low and take steps to recharge. This could involve taking short breaks throughout the day, exercising regularly, or getting enough sleep.
2. **Maintain a Clear Mind**: A cluttered mind is like a dirty windshield, obscuring your view and hampering your ability to navigate effectively. Keep your mind clear through practices like mindfulness, meditation, or simply spending a few quiet moments each day reflecting on your experiences.
3. **Schedule Regular Tune-Ups**: Just as a car needs regular maintenance, your mind and body need regular check-ups, too. This might involve scheduling regular medical check-ups, taking vacations to recharge, or setting aside time each week for activities you enjoy.
4. **Eat a Balanced Diet**: You wouldn't put the wrong fuel in your car, would you? Similarly, nourishing your body with a balanced diet can boost your energy levels and overall well-being.
5. **Stay Connected**: Maintaining solid relationships can boost your mood and provide a support network when facing challenges. Please connect with family and friends, and don't hesitate to seek support.

**The Impact of Self-Care on Leadership Performance**

So, how does self-care tie into leadership performance? Let's go back to our car analogy. A well-maintained car runs more efficiently, performs better, and is less likely to break down. Similarly, a leader who practices regular self-care will likely be more productive, effective, and resilient.

Self-care can boost energy, improve focus, and enhance decision-making skills. It can also improve your emotional intelligence, making you more attuned to your own and your team's emotions.

Moreover, leaders who practice self-care set a positive example for their team. They create a culture where well-being is valued, it's okay to take a break, and people are encouraged to care for their physical and mental health.

In a nutshell, self-care is not a luxury or an indulgence. It's a critical component of resilient leadership. Regular maintenance keeps your engine running smoothly, the fuel that powers your journey, and the driving force behind a healthier, happier, and more resilient you. So, remember to take care of yourself. After all, you can't lead effectively if you're running on empty.

# Building a Resilient Team

### The Importance of Team Resilience

Picture a flock of geese flying in a V formation. Notice how they alternate leaders, share the workload, and support each other through their long journey. This is a perfect example of team resilience.

Much like our flock of geese, team resilience is about collective strength, shared responsibility, and mutual support. A team can withstand challenges, adapt to change, and bounce back stronger.

A resilient team is like a well-built house. It's designed to weather storms, withstand intense winds, and stand tall. It's not about avoiding challenges but about being prepared to face them, knowing that the foundation is strong, the walls are sturdy, and the roof is secure.

Team resilience is crucial in the dynamic business world, where constant change and challenges are inevitable. It can mean the difference between a team that crumbles under pressure and a team that thrives despite it.

**Strategies for Fostering Resilience in Teams: Building the House of Success**

So, how do you construct a resilient team to weather any storm? Let's revisit our house analogy. Building a resilient team is akin to making a sturdy house – it requires a strong foundation, quality materials, and a comprehensive plan. Here are some strategies to help fortify your team's resilience:

1. **Lay a Solid Foundation of Trust:** Trust is the bedrock of a resilient team. Establish an environment where team members can confidently voice their ideas, express concerns, and take calculated risks. When trust is present, collaboration flourishes, and challenges become growth opportunities.

2. **Utilize Robust Materials of Communication and Collaboration:** Open communication and effective collaboration form the robust materials that bind your team together. Foster an atmosphere of transparent dialogue where diverse perspectives are valued and every voice is heard. Encourage teamwork, mutual support, and shared accountability to enhance cohesion and resilience.

3. **Construct with a Solid Plan of Shared Goals and Vision:** A cohesive team is guided by a shared vision and common objectives. Craft a clear roadmap that outlines the team's purpose, goals, and values. Ensure that everyone understands their role in achieving these objectives and feels a sense of ownership in the team's success.

4. **Equip with the Tools of Adaptability and Flexibility:** In the face of adversity or change, these qualities are invaluable. Cultivate a culture that embraces innovation, welcomes challenges as opportunities for growth, and encourages

continuous learning. Equip team members with the skills and mindset to navigate uncertainty and thrive in dynamic environments.

5. **Insulate with a Layer of Recognition and Appreciation:** Recognition and appreciation act as insulation, keeping team morale high and fostering resilience. Acknowledge and celebrate individual and collective achievements, no matter how small. Express gratitude for contributions and efforts to reinforce positive behaviors and strengthen team cohesion.

6. **Maintain Regularly with Feedback and Continuous Improvement:** Just as a house requires regular maintenance to remain structurally sound, a resilient team necessitates ongoing feedback and continuous improvement. Encourage a culture of constructive feedback, where insights are shared openly and used to drive positive change. Foster a growth mindset that values learning, adaptation, and innovation.

With these strategies, you can cultivate resilience within your team, turning it into a well-built house that can withstand any challenge or adversity. Investing in trust, communication, shared purpose, adaptability, recognition, and continuous improvement lays the foundation for a resilient and high-performing team that thrives in the face of adversity.

**Case Studies of Resilient Teams**

Let's look at some examples of resilient teams, much like well-built houses that withstood the test of time.

Consider NASA's Apollo 13 mission control team. When an oxygen tank exploded on the spacecraft, it put the crew's lives in grave danger and threatened the mission's success. However, the ground team at mission control displayed incredible resilience. They remained calm under pressure, worked together to solve the problem, and ultimately devised a plan that brought the crew safely back to Earth.

Another example is the All Blacks, New Zealand's national rugby team, known for their remarkable resilience. Despite the high-pressure nature of international rugby, the team maintains a winning record through a culture of psychological safety, mutual trust, and a shared commitment to excellence.

In both cases, the teams faced significant challenges and high-stress situations. Yet they navigated these difficulties through their resilience. They demonstrate how trust, communication, a shared vision, adaptability, recognition, and continuous improvement can form a resilient team.

So, whether you're navigating a crisis in space, facing a formidable opponent on the rugby field, or leading a team in the corporate world, remember this: Building a resilient team is like constructing a well-built house. It requires a strong foundation, sturdy materials, and regular maintenance. It's not an overnight process but an ongoing project. But with patience, persistence, and the right strategies, you can build a team that stands tall, weathers storms, and shines brightly, even on the cloudiest days.

As we conclude this chapter, remember that personal and collective resilience are critical to effective leadership. It's about bouncing back from challenges, turning setbacks into comebacks, and fostering a team culture where everyone feels safe, supported, and inspired to do their best. So, let's continue cultivating resilience in ourselves and our teams. When we rise to challenges, learn from setbacks, and bounce back more robustly, we build resilience and character, forge bonds, and lead toward a more resilient, firmer, and radiant future.

With this chapter's insights into our leadership toolkit, let's continue our exploration. As we turn the page to the next chapter, we will delve into the vibrant realm of inclusive leadership, exploring its many facets and discovering how we can foster a culture of inclusion, empathy, and mutual respect in our teams. Let's continue this enlightening journey, embracing the lessons, celebrating the milestones, and looking forward to the exciting adventures that still await us.

# Chapter Summary

Resilience is likened to a rubber ball's ability to rebound from impact, a quality essential for leaders facing challenges. The chapter explores the definition of resilience, delves into the science behind it, and offers practical strategies for building personal resilience.

**Key Points:**

- **Defining Resilience:** Resilience is the refusal to be reduced by adversity. Leadership involves staying focused, maintaining conviction, and leading with determination despite uncertainties.
- **The Science of Resilience:** Resilience is influenced by both genetics and learned skills. Traits like optimism, a sense of purpose, and strong social connections contribute to resilience. Regular practice and a positive mindset can enhance resilience.
- **Strategies for Building Personal Resilience:** Practical strategies include cultivating a positive mindset, fostering strong relationships, embracing change, caring for health, and setting realistic goals. Building resilience is a continuous journey.
- **Leveraging Failure:** Failure is explored as a teacher who challenges, tests, and cultivates resilience. Case studies of leaders like Steve Jobs and Arianna Huffington demonstrate how failure can lead to tremendous success.
- **The Role of Self-Care:** The connection between self-care and resilience is highlighted. Practical self-care strategies are discussed, such as monitoring energy levels, maintaining a clear mind, scheduling regular tune-ups, eating a balanced diet, and staying connected.

- **Building a Resilient Team:** Team resilience is compared to a well-built house designed to withstand challenges. Strategies for fostering team resilience include establishing trust, promoting communication and collaboration, defining shared goals, embracing adaptability, recognizing and appreciating team members, and maintaining regular feedback and continuous improvement.
- **Case Studies of Resilient Teams:** Examples include NASA's Apollo 13 mission control team and the All-Blacks rugby team. Trust, communication, shared vision, adaptability, recognition, and continuous improvement contribute to team resilience.

The chapter concludes by emphasizing the critical role of personal and collective resilience in effective leadership. It encourages the continuous cultivation of resilience in individuals and teams, highlighting its impact on character-building and leading towards a more robust and radiant future.

As the leadership journey unfolds, the next chapter will explore inclusive leadership, delving into its facets and showing how to foster a culture of inclusion, empathy, and mutual respect in teams.

# EIGHT

# THE INCLUSIVE SYMPHONY
## CONDUCTING A
## HARMONIOUS WORKPLACE

Use vivid metaphors like attending a symphony to draw readers into the concept of psychological safety, making the idea memorable and engaging.

## The Importance of Psychological Safety

### Defining Psychological Safety

Psychological safety is about trust and mutual respect, like the bond between orchestra members. When team members trust that they can speak up and be authentic, they feel reassured and safe, which is essential for their engagement and well-being.

### The Role of Psychological Safety in Inclusion

In the orchestra of inclusivity, psychological safety is the harmonious melody that binds all different notes together. It's the foundation upon which diversity thrives and inclusion blossoms. When team members feel psychologically safe, they're more likely to share their unique perspectives, contribute diverse ideas, and collaborate effectively. It's like creating a symphony where each musician, no matter their instrument, feels heard, valued, and included.

Emphasize that Google's research shows that psychological safety directly impacts innovation and performance, encouraging leaders to act.

**Strategies for Fostering Psychological Safety**

Frame strategies as essential tools for leaders to conduct their team's symphony, emphasizing their role in fostering psychological safety.

1. **Encourage Open Communication**: Just as a conductor invites each musician to play their part, encourage team members to voice their thoughts, ideas, and concerns. Ensure that all opinions are valued and feedback is welcomed and appreciated.
2. **Show Vulnerability**: As a leader, showing vulnerability can be powerful. Admitting your own mistakes or uncertainties fosters approachability, making others feel more connected and comfortable doing the same. It's like a conductor admitting they missed a beat; it humanizes them and builds trust.
3. **Promote a Learning Culture**: Foster an environment that values curiosity, questions, and learning from mistakes. Rather than seeing errors as failures, view them as opportunities for learning and growth. It's like a missed note becoming a chance for a musician to improve.
4. **Lead with Empathy**: Show understanding and compassion towards your team members. Recognize their challenges, validate their feelings, and offer support. Just as a conductor empathizes with a musician facing a problematic passage, your empathy can help build a psychologically safe space.
5. **Set an Example**: Model the behavior you want to see. Communicate openly, admit your own mistakes, ask for

feedback, and show respect for all team members. Your actions set the tone for the team, just like a conductor's baton guides the orchestra.

Remember, creating psychological safety is like tuning an orchestra. It requires attention, fine-tuning, and ongoing effort. But the result - a team that trusts one another, communicates openly, and feels safe to express their unique voices - is worth every effort. After all, that's how the most beautiful symphonies are created.

# Promoting Allyship in the Workplace

### Understanding Allyship

Imagine you're a gardener, nurturing diverse plants. Each plant has unique needs - some need more sunlight; others thrive in the shade. As a gardener, your role is to understand these needs and provide the right environment for each plant to thrive. Allyship, in many ways, is similar to this.

Allyship is about recognizing the diverse needs, experiences, and struggles of others and using your privilege to support and advocate for them. It's about standing up for those who are marginalized or underrepresented, even when it's uncomfortable or challenging. Like the gardener who waters the plants in the shadowy corners, an ally ensures everyone has an equal opportunity to grow.

### The Role of Allyship in Inclusive Leadership

In the orchestra of inclusive leadership, allies are like the supporting musicians who amplify the soloists, ensuring that every note and melody is heard and appreciated.

An inclusive leader who practices allyship actively works towards creating an equitable workplace. They strive to understand their team members' unique challenges, particularly those from underrepresented or marginalized groups. They actively work to dismantle the barriers these team members face and amplify their voices.

They also challenge biases and discriminatory behaviors in themselves and their team. They're not afraid to speak up against injustice and to take action to promote inclusion and equality. It's like a conductor who ensures that every musician has an equal opportunity to shine, no matter their instrument.

**Steps to Becoming an Effective Ally**

Becoming an effective ally is like learning a new piece of music. It requires practice, patience, and a willingness to learn. Here are some steps to help you play the allyship symphony:

1. **Educate Yourself**: Just like a musician who studies the score before picking up their instrument, try to learn about the experiences, struggles, and needs of different groups. Read books, attend workshops, listen to podcasts, and stay informed.
2. **Listen and Learn**: Be open to listening to and learning from others' experiences. Understand that their experiences may differ from yours, and that's okay. It's like appreciating the unique melodies of different instruments.
3. **Speak Up**: Use your voice to challenge bias, discrimination, and unfair treatment. It can be uncomfortable, but remember that silence can often be seen as complicity. It's like a musician playing a wrong note - it's essential to correct it, not ignore it.
4. **Take Action**: Allyship is not just about words; it's about actions. Advocate for policies that promote equality and inclusion. Support initiatives that uplift marginalized groups. It's like a conductor, not just directing the music but actively shaping the performance.
5. **Keep Learning**: Allyship is a continuous process. Keep educating yourself, listening, challenging your biases, and

working towards creating a more inclusive and equitable workplace. It's like a musician who never stops practicing, knowing there's always room for improvement.

In conclusion, allyship is a crucial component of inclusive leadership. It's about actively promoting equality, standing up for justice, and creating a workplace where everyone feels seen, heard, and valued. So, let's strive to be allies, amplifying the voices that need to be heard and playing our part in the symphony of inclusion. Because when we do, we're not just making beautiful music; we're making a difference.

# Leading by Example: Modeling Inclusive Behavior

### The Power of Leading by Example

Imagine a conductor standing before an orchestra. With each flick of the baton, a different section of the orchestra comes to life, mirroring the conductor's movements. This is the power of leading by example.

Inclusive leaders, like conductors, set the tempo for their teams through their actions. They don't just discuss diversity and inclusion; they demonstrate it in their behavior. They respect all team members, value everyone's contributions, and prioritize fairness in decision-making. They make a point of listening, understanding, and empathizing.

Leading by example is more than just a leadership strategy; it's a way of life. It's about embodying the values you promote, living the principles you uphold, and becoming a living, breathing testament to the power of inclusive leadership.

### Strategies for Modeling Inclusive Behavior

So, how does one lead by example? Here are some strategies to help you set the tempo for inclusive behavior:

1. **Be a Role Model for Respect**: Treat everyone in your team with dignity and respect, regardless of their role, background, or identity. Make sure your actions reflect this principle at all times.
2. **Encourage Diverse Perspectives**: Actively seek out and value diverse viewpoints. Show your team that every voice matters and that different perspectives are a strength, not a threat.
3. **Practice Fair Decision-Making**: Make decisions based on fairness and merit, not favoritism or bias. When your team sees that their hard work and contributions are recognized and rewarded fairly, they're more likely to trust and respect your leadership.
4. **Communicate Openly and Transparently**: Be open about your decision-making process and keep your team informed about important issues. This level of transparency can create trust and make everyone feel included.
5. **Show Empathy and Understanding**: Demonstrate understanding and empathy in your interactions with your team. You create a supportive and inclusive environment when you show that you care about their feelings and experiences.
6. **Champion Diversity and Inclusion Initiatives**: Demonstrate your commitment to diversity and inclusion by actively supporting initiatives that advance them. This could be anything from diversity training programs to inclusive hiring practices.

Remember, leading by example is like conducting an orchestra. Your actions set the tone, your behavior influences the performance, and your commitment to inclusion inspires the symphony of teamwork.

### The Impact of Inclusive Leadership on Team Dynamics

Now, let's consider the impact of inclusive leadership on team dynamics. Picture a choir where every member feels confident to sing their part, knowing their voice adds to the harmony. This is the kind of dynamic that inclusive leadership can foster.

When leaders model inclusive behavior, they create a team culture where everyone feels valued, heard, and included. This can boost team morale, enhance collaboration, and increase productivity.

Inclusive leadership can also foster innovation. When everyone feels safe to express their ideas, the team can tap into a broader range of perspectives, leading to more creative and innovative solutions.

Moreover, inclusive leadership can enhance team resilience. Teams that feel valued and included are more likely to support one another during challenging times, thereby improving their collective ability to bounce back from setbacks.

In short, inclusive leadership, modeled through leading by example, can transform team dynamics. It's like a maestro conducting an orchestra, bringing out the best in each musician, creating a harmonious performance, and captivating the audience with a symphony of inclusion.

## The Impact of Inclusive Leadership on Organizational Culture

### The Connection Between Inclusive Leadership and Organizational Culture

Imagine a garden where every plant is nurtured, every flower blooms in its own unique way, and diversity is celebrated - the kind of environment inclusive leadership can cultivate in an organization.

Inclusive leadership is like sunlight and rain, enabling the garden to flourish. It permeates every aspect of an organization, shaping its culture, influencing its values, and guiding its practices. When leaders demonstrate inclusivity, they create a culture that values diversity, promotes equality, and fosters a sense of belonging.

Just as a garden's health is reflected in the vibrancy of its plants, an organization's culture is mirrored in the engagement, productivity, and satisfaction of its employees. An inclusive culture attracts a diverse workforce and enables them to thrive and contribute to their fullest potential.

**Case Studies of Inclusive Organizational Cultures**

Consider the case of a global technology company, Microsoft. Under the leadership of CEO Satya Nadella, the company made a significant shift towards a more inclusive culture. This involved fostering a 'growth mindset,' promoting diversity, and nurturing a culture where every employee feels valued and heard. The outcome? A surge in innovation, employee engagement, and business performance.

Similarly, multinational consumer goods corporation Procter & Gamble has been recognized for its commitment to inclusion. The company has implemented various initiatives - from diversity training programs to inclusive hiring practices - to create a culture where everyone feels they belong. As a result, the company has seen increased employee retention, greater innovation, and expanded market reach.

These examples illustrate the powerful impact of inclusive leadership on organizational culture. They show leaders committed to fostering inclusion can transform the workplace, driving innovation, engagement, and performance.

**Strategies for Shaping an Inclusive Organizational Culture**

So, how can a leader shape an inclusive organizational culture? Here are a few strategies akin to a gardener tending to their garden, ensuring every plant has the opportunity to thrive:

1. **Promote Inclusive Values**: Clearly articulate and consistently uphold the organization's commitment to diversity and inclusion. This sets the tone for the entire organization and sends a clear message about what is valued.

2. **Champion Diversity and Inclusion Initiatives**: Support and participate in these initiatives. This demonstrates leadership commitment and can inspire others to get involved.
3. **Foster an Open and Safe Environment**: Create a workplace where everyone feels safe to express their thoughts, ideas, and concerns without fear of reprisal. This fosters open dialogue, mutual respect, and a sense of belonging.
4. **Encourage Diverse Perspectives**: Value and seek out diverse perspectives when making decisions. This leads to better decision-making and powerfully conveys that all voices are valued.
5. **Model Inclusive Behaviors**: Leaders play a crucial role in setting the standard for workplace behavior. By modeling inclusive behavior, leaders can influence others to do the same.

Creating an inclusive organizational culture is not a one-time project but an ongoing commitment. It requires persistence, patience, and a genuine commitment to diversity and inclusion. But the result - a vibrant, inclusive culture where everyone feels valued and can thrive - is undoubtedly worth the effort.

As we wrap up this chapter, let's remember that inclusive leadership, like a gardener tending to a garden, plays a crucial role in cultivating an inclusive organizational culture. It's about nurturing every 'plant,' enabling them to bloom uniquely and together, creating a diverse, vibrant, and flourishing garden. So, as we continue our exploration in the next chapter, let's carry the insights, lessons, and strategies we've gleaned, ready to cultivate our gardens of inclusive leadership.

# Chapter Summary

This chapter employs the metaphor of a symphony orchestra to convey the essence of psychological safety, allyship, leading by example, and their impact on team dynamics and organizational culture.

The chapter begins by likening a workplace to a symphony, emphasizing the need for each member to feel safe in expressing their unique contributions and fostering psychological safety. Psychological safety, defined as trust and mutual respect, is depicted as the harmonious melody binding diversity in an inclusive workplace. The chapter highlights the pivotal role of psychological safety in promoting innovation, team learning, and overall performance.

Allyship is then introduced through the analogy of a gardener nurturing diverse plants. The concept involves recognizing others' needs, leveraging privilege to support them, and actively working toward equity. Allyship in inclusive leadership involves actively dismantling barriers and amplifying underrepresented voices.

The section on leading by example likens inclusive leaders to conductors setting the tempo for their teams. Strategies for modeling inclusive behavior are outlined, emphasizing respect, diverse perspectives, fair decision-making, open communication, empathy, and championing diversity initiatives.

The impact of inclusive leadership on team dynamics is likened to a choir where every member confidently contributes, fostering collaboration, productivity, innovation, and resilience. The subsequent section extends this impact to organizational culture, drawing parallels with a flourishing garden. Case studies of Microsoft and Procter & Gamble illustrate how inclusive leadership can transform corporate cultures, leading to increased innovation, engagement, and performance.

The chapter concludes with strategies for shaping an inclusive organizational culture, promoting inclusive values, championing diversity initiatives, fostering a safe environment, encouraging diverse perspectives, and modeling inclusive behaviors. The ongoing commitment required to create an inclusive culture is akin to a gardener's persistence and patience.

As the chapter concludes, readers are encouraged to carry the insights, lessons, and strategies learned into the next chapter, ready to cultivate their gardens of inclusive leadership.

# NINE

## THE STRATEGIST
## AND THE ALCHEMIST

### WOMEN LEADERS IN THE
### CHANGING LANDSCAPE OF WORK

Picture yourself as a strategist on a chessboard, carefully observing the game, considering all potential moves, and strategizing your next step. Now, morph that image into an alchemist, transforming the ordinary into the extraordinary, turning lead into gold. My dear reader, this duality represents the modern woman leader - part strategist, part alchemist-navigating the ever-evolving landscape of work and shaping a golden future.

## Women Leaders and the
## Changing Landscape of Work

### The Evolving Workplace and Its Impact on Women Leaders

The workplace is like a kaleidoscope, continuously shifting and presenting new patterns and perspectives. Technological advancements, societal changes, and global events are turning the dial, leading to significant transformations in our work.

For instance, the rise of remote work has been a significant shift. Just like a home office can exist anywhere from a spare room to a cozy corner of the living room, work is no longer confined to the four walls of an office. This increased flexibility can be a double-edged sword for women leaders. On the one hand, it can provide a greater work-life balance and eliminate commute-related stress. On the other hand, it can blur the boundaries between professional and personal life, leading to longer working hours and increased stress.

Another significant shift is the growing importance of emotional intelligence in leadership. In a remote work environment, leaders must be attuned to their team's emotional well-being, even without face-to-face interactions. This shift plays to the strengths of many women leaders, who often excel in empathy and emotional understanding.

### The Role of Women Leaders in Shaping the Future of Work

In the ever-evolving landscape of work, women leaders are not just players but architects, actively shaping the future of work. They are like the alchemists of old, transforming the raw materials of today's workplace into a golden future.

As architects, women leaders champion flexibility, advocating for policies that support work-life balance. They pave the way for more inclusive workplaces where diversity is valued, and everyone's contributions are recognized, fueling a sense of purpose.

Moreover, women leaders leverage their emotional intelligence to create supportive work environments. They foster open communication, promote mental health, and build teams where everyone feels appreciated and motivated.

### Case Studies of Women Leaders Navigating Change

Let's look at some real-life alchemists and strategists, women leaders who have successfully navigated change and shaped the future of work.

Consider Indra Nooyi, the former CEO of PepsiCo. Under her leadership, PepsiCo transformed its product portfolio, expanded globally, and doubled its revenue. Nooyi's leadership style, characterized by long-term strategic thinking and a focus on employee well-being, played a significant role in this transformation.

Next, let's turn our attention to Mary Barra, the CEO of General Motors. She has been instrumental in steering the company towards electric vehicles and autonomous driving technology. Her strategic foresight and commitment to innovation shape the future of General Motors and the entire automotive industry.

These examples illustrate how women leaders, through strategic thinking and a touch of alchemy, navigate change and shape the future of work. They remind us that leadership is not just about reacting to change but proactively creating it. It's about turning the chessboard, shifting the kaleidoscope, and architecting a future where everyone can thrive.

# The Role of Women Leaders in Driving Innovation

### Women Leaders as Innovators: Shaping the Future with Creativity and Vision

Imagine a sculptor standing before a raw block of marble, envisioning the masterpiece that lies within. With each precise stroke of the chisel, she brings her vision to life, transforming the ordinary into the extraordinary. In the same way, women leaders are the architects of innovation, sculpting the future with their creativity and vision.

Women leaders possess a unique ability to challenge the status quo and drive meaningful change. Like the sculptor's chisel, they wield their insight and expertise to carve out fresh perspectives, refine processes, and pioneer groundbreaking initiatives. Their innovative spirit knows no bounds as they navigate uncharted territories and push the boundaries of what is possible.

In every industry and sector, women leaders are at the forefront of innovation, harnessing their diverse perspectives and experiences to spark transformative ideas. Whether in technology, finance, healthcare, or beyond, they are catalysts for progress, driving advancements that shape our world.

Take, for example, the traditionally male-dominated tech industry. Women leaders are not merely participants but trailblazers, driving innovation at every turn. They are the driving force behind cutting-edge technologies, pioneering new business models, and revolutionizing the digital landscape. From AI and cybersecurity to e-commerce and biotech, women leaders are leaving an indelible mark on the future of technology.

Moreover, women leaders bring a holistic approach to innovation, recognizing the importance of diversity, inclusivity, and sustainability. They understand that true innovation extends beyond mere technological advancement; it encompasses social impact, environmental stewardship, and ethical leadership. By embracing these values, women leaders are shaping the future of their organizations and creating a more equitable and sustainable world for generations to come.

In essence, women leaders are the visionary sculptors of our time, chiseling away at the barriers of conventionality to reveal the brilliance that lies beneath. With their ingenuity, resilience, and unwavering determination, they are reshaping industries, driving progress, and inspiring a new era of innovation. As we look to the future, let us celebrate and empower women leaders as the driving force behind transformative change and endless possibilities.

### The Impact of Women Leaders on Organizational Innovation: Catalyzing Change and Driving Success

Imagine a tranquil pond, its surface undisturbed until a single stone is thrown, creating ripples reverberating across its expanse. Similarly, the impact of women leaders on organizational innovation sends forth waves of transformation, touching every facet of the workplace with their ingenuity and vision.

Research unequivocally demonstrates that companies led by women in top management positions exhibit heightened levels of innovation and superior financial performance. This correlation is not fate; instead, it is a testament to the unique contributions of women leaders in fostering a culture of creativity and progress.

Research unequivocally demonstrates that companies led by women in top management positions exhibit heightened levels of innovation and superior financial performance. This is a direct result of women leaders challenging conventional thinking and embracing fresh viewpoints, which injects vitality into organizational dynamics and spurs success.

Moreover, women leaders possess a remarkable aptitude for cultivating inclusive work environments where every voice is heard and valued. By championing open communication, embracing diverse opinions, and fostering collaboration, they lay the foundation for innovation to flourish. In such environments, ideas are freely exchanged, barriers are dismantled, and collective creativity blossoms.

Furthermore, women leaders excel at nurturing talent and empowering individuals to unleash their full potential. They cultivate a workforce primed to innovate and adapt to evolving challenges by prioritizing mentorship, coaching, and professional development initiatives. Through their leadership, women inspire confidence, resilience, and a relentless pursuit of excellence, driving organizational innovation to new heights.

In essence, the impact of women leaders on organizational innovation transcends mere statistics; it is a testament to the transformative power of diversity, inclusion, and visionary leadership. As they chart new paths, challenge the status quo, and inspire those around them, women leaders are catalysts for change, driving organizations toward a future of innovation, growth, and enduring success.

**Strategies for Fostering Innovation as a Woman Leader: Cultivating the Seeds of Change**

Fostering innovation as a woman leader is akin to tending a garden. This delicate yet transformative process requires patience, dedication, and a keen understanding of what it takes to nurture growth. Here are some strategies to help you cultivate innovation within your team:

1. **Cultivate a Safe Space for Ideas to Flourish:** Just as a garden thrives in a nurturing environment, innovation flourishes in a culture that welcomes and celebrates ideas. Create a safe space where team members feel empowered to share their thoughts and insights, regardless of how unconventional they may seem. Encourage an atmosphere of trust and openness, where every idea is allowed to take root and grow.

2. **Embrace the Diversity of Perspectives:** Diversity is the lifeblood of innovation, much like the array of plants in a thriving garden. Embrace and celebrate the diverse perspectives within your team, recognizing that each viewpoint brings a unique contribution. Encourage collaboration across different backgrounds, experiences, and skill sets, acknowledging that it is through this diversity that the most innovative ideas often emerge.

3. **Cultivate a Culture of Continuous Learning and Experimentation:** Innovation thrives in an environment where learning is prized and experimentation is encouraged. Encourage your team to embrace a growth mindset, viewing failure not as a setback but as an opportunity for learning and growth. Just as a garden requires regular pruning and weeding, innovation also benefits from a willingness to iterate, refine, and evolve.

4. **Lead with Curiosity and Openness:** As a leader, you set the tone for innovation within your team. Lead by example, demonstrating a genuine curiosity for new ideas and a willingness to challenge the status quo. Foster an environment where curiosity is celebrated, questions are welcomed, and everyone feels empowered to contribute their unique perspective. By leading with openness and a spirit of inquiry,

you inspire your team to do the same, laying the groundwork for a culture of innovation to flourish.

As a woman leader, you possess a unique opportunity to drive innovation within your organization. By embracing these strategies and cultivating a culture that values creativity and collaboration, you can unleash your team's full potential and pave the way for groundbreaking ideas to take root and thrive. So, roll up your sleeves, dig in, and let's cultivate a future where innovation knows no bounds.

# Women Leaders Shaping Policy and Governance

### Women Leaders in Policy and Governance Roles

Imagine a roundtable buzzing with animated conversations, thoughtful insights, and visionary ideas. Now, picture women leaders taking their rightful seats at this table, their voices resonating, their influence rippling through policy and governance.

Women leaders bring unique perspectives, insights, and experiences in policymaking and governance. They're not just participants in the dialogue but instigators of change, catalysts for progress, and architects of a more equitable future.

Whether in government, non-profit organizations, or corporate boards, women leaders influence policymaking and governance at multiple levels. They advocate for equitable laws, promote sustainable practices, and champion social justice. They shape organizational strategies, influence industry standards, and drive systemic change.

### The Impact of Women Leaders on Policy and Governance

The impact of women leaders on policy and governance is akin to the ripple effect of a pebble thrown into a pond. Their influence extends beyond their immediate roles, affecting broader organizational strategies, industry practices, and societal norms.

Women leaders bring a fresh perspective to policymaking and governance, often prioritizing inclusivity, sustainability, and social responsibility. Their approach tends to be more collaborative, empathetic, and holistic. They understand the interconnectedness of issues and consider the broader implications of policies and decisions.

Including women in policymaking and governance roles also promotes diversity and representation. It ensures that diverse perspectives are considered and that policies and decisions are more equitable and inclusive.

Moreover, women leaders often use their influence to champion issues that may be overlooked, such as gender equality, social justice, and environmental sustainability. They're not just shaping policies and governance; they're reshaping the narrative, challenging the status quo, and driving societal progress.

### Case Studies of Women Leaders Influencing Policy and Governance

Let's spotlight a few women leaders who have significantly contributed to policy and governance.

Consider Jacinda Ardern, the Prime Minister of New Zealand. Under her leadership, New Zealand has implemented progressive policies on climate change, child poverty, and gun control. Ardern's empathetic and decisive leadership style, particularly in times of crisis, has been widely applauded. She has prioritized people and well-being in her policies, demonstrating the potential impact of women leaders in policy-making roles.

Similarly, Ruth Bader Ginsburg, the late Supreme Court Justice in the United States, used her role to champion equality and social justice. She was crucial in landmark rulings that advanced gender equality, women's rights, and civil liberties. Her relentless pursuit of justice and equality reshaped American law and society, underscoring the significant influence of women leaders in governance.

Closer to home, in the corporate world, Mary Barra, the CEO of General Motors, has been instrumental in steering the company towards more sustainable practices. Under her leadership, General Motors has committed to producing only electric vehicles by 2035, a significant policy shift expected to drive industry-wide change.

These women leaders, with their strategic minds and alchemist spirits, remind us of women's powerful impact on policy and governance. They inspire us to step up, speak out, and take our rightful seats at the table. They show us that leadership is not just about holding a position but about making a difference. They challenge us not just to play the game but to change it. Most importantly, they motivate us to dream of a better future and actively shape it.

So, as we navigate the intricate maze of leadership, let's carry with us the lessons we've learned, the inspiration we've gained, and the determination we've forged. Remember that we are not just strategists on a chessboard or alchemists in a lab; we are architects of change, visionaries of progress, and future sculptors. And with every policy we influence, every decision we make, and every action we take, we're not just leading; we're transforming the work landscape, one golden move at a time.

# Preparing the Next Generation of Women Leaders: Nurturing Growth Through Mentorship and Sponsorship

### The Importance of Mentorship and Sponsorship: Guiding Lights on the Path to Leadership

Reflect for a moment on your first bicycle ride without training wheels. Perhaps a trusted individual steadied the bike, ran alongside you, and let go when you found your balance. This guiding presence is reminiscent of a mentor in the professional realm.

In the intricate landscape of leadership, mentorship holds a profound significance. Mentors, seasoned leaders with a wealth of experience, offer guidance, share knowledge, and provide invaluable insights gleaned from their journeys. For emerging women leaders, a mentor can serve as a wellspring of inspiration, a safe harbor for ideas, and a lighthouse guiding them through uncharted waters.

On the other hand, sponsorship embodies advocacy. Sponsors and influential figures within an organization leverage their positions to propel the careers of their protégés. They are akin to the wind beneath the wings of aspiring leaders, pushing them upward in the professional sphere.

For emerging women leaders, having a sponsor can unlock doors, amplify their voices, and grant access to opportunities that might otherwise remain elusive. In the grand tapestry of leadership development, sponsors are the maestros who showcase their protégés' talents, illuminating them for the world to see.

**Enhancing Mentorship and Sponsorship: Empowering the Leaders of Tomorrow**

To prepare the next generation of women leaders, it is imperative to foster robust mentorship and sponsorship programs that empower growth and development. Here's how:

1. **Cultivate Meaningful Mentorship Relationships:**
   Encourage emerging leaders to seek mentors who align with their aspirations and values. Facilitate meaningful connections between mentors and mentees, providing a platform for knowledge sharing, skill development, and personal growth.
2. **Champion Sponsorship Initiatives:** Actively identify and cultivate sponsors within your organization who are committed to championing the careers of emerging women leaders. Encourage sponsors to advocate for their protégés,

give them visibility and opportunities for advancement, and actively support their professional growth.

3. **Foster a Culture of Paying It Forward:** Encourage women leaders to pay forward the support and guidance they receive by becoming mentors and sponsors. Emphasize the importance of lifting others as they climb and creating a ripple effect of empowerment and advancement within the organization.

By prioritizing mentorship and sponsorship initiatives, organizations can nurture the next generation of women leaders, equipping them with the skills, support, and opportunities they need to thrive. Together, let's pave the way for a future where leadership knows no gender and every aspiring leader has the guidance and support they need to soar.

**Strategies for Developing Future Women Leaders: Nurturing the Seeds of Leadership**

Cultivating the next generation of women leaders is akin to tending seeds, nurturing them into resilient, flourishing plants. It requires deliberate attention, promotes care, and creates an environment conducive to growth. Here are several strategies to help these seeds of leadership thrive:

1. **Cultivate a Culture of Leadership Development:** Celebrate growth and development at all levels. Encourage aspiring leaders to step into leadership roles by providing opportunities to lead projects, initiatives, or teams. Foster an environment where leadership is seen as a continuous learning and improvement journey.

2. **Provide Accessible Training and Development Programs:** Offer accessible and tailored leadership training and development programs. These initiatives should equip emerging leaders with the skills, knowledge, and confidence needed to

navigate the complexities of leadership. Consider offering both formal training sessions and informal mentorship opportunities to accommodate different learning styles and preferences.

3. **Facilitate Networking Opportunities:** Help aspiring women leaders within and outside the organization connect and network. Networking provides invaluable exposure to diverse perspectives, leadership styles, and industry insights. Encourage participation in professional associations, conferences, and industry events to expand networks and forge meaningful connections.

4. **Foster a Culture of Feedback and Growth:** Encourage continuous feedback and growth, with individuals seeking and providing constructive feedback. Feedback nourishes growth, offering valuable insights and opportunities for improvement. Encourage leaders at all levels to prioritize regular feedback exchanges and create a safe space for open dialogue and reflection.

5. **Cultivate a Supportive and Inclusive Environment:** Create an inclusive environment where emerging leaders feel empowered to take risks, express their ideas, and contribute authentically. Ensure that organizational policies, practices, and behaviors are committed to diversity, equity, and inclusion. By fostering a culture of belonging and respect, organizations can create fertile ground for the growth and development of future women leaders.

By implementing these strategies, organizations can actively cultivate the next generation of women leaders, nurturing their potential and empowering them to thrive in leadership roles. Just as careful cultivation leads to a bountiful harvest, investing in the development of future women leaders will yield long-lasting benefits for individuals, organizations, and society.

**The Role of Current Women Leaders in Shaping the Next Generation**

Current women leaders play a crucial role in shaping the next generation. They are the gardeners who water the saplings, prune the branches, and protect them from the harsh elements.

As role models, they embody practical leadership qualities and inspire the next generation through their actions. As mentors and sponsors, they provide guidance, share their wisdom, and advocate for their protégés. As advocates for diversity and inclusion, they pave the way for future women leaders, breaking down barriers and challenging biases.

In essence, current women leaders are not just leading their teams or organizations; they are shaping the future of leadership. They are ensuring that the next generation of women leaders is equipped, empowered, and ready to take on the challenges and opportunities that lie ahead.

Each generation of women leaders is a chapter in the grand narrative of leadership. And as we pen our chapter, we also have the privilege of shaping the following chapters. We have the opportunity to pass the baton, share our wisdom, and ensure that the next generation of women leaders is ready to run the race.

As we wrap up this chapter, remember that we are not just strategists and alchemists but also mentors, sponsors, and role models. We are not just shaping the present but also the future. We lead, inspire, guide, and empower the next generation of women leaders. In doing so, we are creating a ripple effect that will resonate far beyond our leadership journey, creating a symphony of leadership that will echo through the ages.

As we turn the page to the next chapter, let's carry the insights we've gleaned, the inspiration we've gathered, and the resolve we've forged. Armed with these, let's continue our exploration, ready to delve deeper, soar higher, and shine brighter in our quest to master the art of inclusive leadership.

# Chapter Summary

This chapter explores the multifaceted role of modern women leaders, portraying them as part strategists and part alchemists. The metaphor of a chessboard strategist and an alchemist transforming the ordinary into the extraordinary depicts women leaders navigating the evolving workplace.

The chapter delves into the impact of technological advancements, societal changes, and global events on the workplace, using the metaphor of a kaleidoscope. The rise of remote work is discussed, highlighting its potential benefits and challenges for women leaders. The importance of emotional intelligence in leadership, especially in a remote work environment, is emphasized, aligning with the strengths of many women leaders.

Women leaders are portrayed as architects shaping the future of work, championing flexibility, advocating for inclusive workplaces, and leveraging emotional intelligence. Real-life case studies of female leaders, such as Indra Nooyi and Mary Barra, illustrate their strategic thinking and alchemical influence in navigating change and shaping the future of work.

The chapter extends to discuss the role of women leaders in driving innovation. Women leaders are compared to sculptors, carving out fresh ideas, fine-tuning processes, and transforming their organizations. The impact of women leaders on organizational innovation is likened to ripples spreading across a pond, influencing diverse perspectives, and fostering a culture of innovation.

Strategies for fostering innovation as a woman leader are outlined, emphasizing the creation of a safe space for ideas, the encouragement of diverse perspectives, the promotion of a culture of learning and experimentation, and leadership with curiosity and openness.

The final sections of the chapter explore the role of women leaders in policy and governance, highlighting their influence in advocating for equitable laws, promoting sustainability, and championing social justice. Case studies of female leaders such as Jacinda Ardern, Ruth Bader Ginsburg, and Mary Barra illustrate the significant impact female leaders can have in policy and governance roles.

The chapter concludes by emphasizing the importance of mentorship and sponsorship in developing future women leaders. Strategies for nurturing the next generation of women leaders are outlined, including fostering a culture of leadership development, providing training opportunities, encouraging networking, offering constructive feedback, and creating a supportive environment.

Current women leaders are depicted as crucial in shaping the next generation, acting as role models, mentors, sponsors, and advocates for diversity and inclusion. The chapter closes by highlighting that women leaders are shaping the present, inspiring and empowering the next generation, creating a ripple effect that resonates through the ages.

As readers turn the page to the next chapter, they are encouraged to carry the insights, inspiration, and resolve gained from this exploration, ready to delve deeper into mastering the art of inclusive leadership.

# TEN

## EUREKA! EXTRACTING GOLD FROM CHAOS

### THE ALCHEMY OF WOMEN'S LEADERSHIP

Let's imagine we're standing at the peak of a high mountain. We've hiked a challenging trail, faced unexpected weather, stumbled over rocks, and maybe even questioned why we thought this was a promising idea in the first place. But here we are, at the summit, taking in the breathtaking view, the fresh air, and the sweet victory. This is a bit like our leadership journey so far. We've navigated the complexities of leadership, tackled challenges, and uncovered insights. We've taken the chaos we started with and, piece by piece, transformed it into gold.

As we catch our breath and take in the panorama, it's a good time to reflect on the path we've traversed. It's a moment to appreciate our personal growth, revisit the lessons learned, and understand the impact of this leadership journey on our personal and professional development.

## Reflection: Looking Back at the Journey

### Reflecting on Personal Growth

Think about the first day of our hike. We were enthusiastic, armed with a map, and probably nervous about the climb. Now, compare that with the person standing at the summit. We're more robust and experienced, and our confidence levels have soared. This transformation reflects our personal growth.

Our leadership journey has been a similar uphill climb. Remember the first day you stepped into a leadership role? The doubts, the excitement, the anticipation? Now look at the leader you've become. You've grown in confidence, honed your skills, and developed an inclusive leadership style that values diversity and promotes equity. Consider which specific inclusive practices, like active listening or bias mitigation, you've integrated to deepen your impact.

Take a moment to jot down the key areas where you've seen personal growth. Maybe you've become more assertive, improved your decision-making skills, or become a better listener. Reflect on how these changes have influenced your ability to foster inclusion and equity within your team. Recognizing these areas helps you build on your strengths and identify opportunities for further growth.

**Lessons Learned from Challenges and Successes**

Every stumble on our hike taught us something. Perhaps we learned to watch our steps more carefully, pace ourselves better, or pack lighter for the journey ahead. Each challenge we faced, each success we celebrated, was a lesson learned.

The same applies to our leadership journey. Every challenge we faced – whether it was balancing multiple roles, overcoming bias, or promoting diversity – taught us valuable lessons about resilience, empathy, and inclusive leadership. Each success, each milestone achieved, offered insights into what works and where we excel. Reflecting on these can inspire confidence and motivate continued growth.

Take a moment to reflect on the challenges you faced and the successes you celebrated. What lessons did they teach you? What insights did they offer?

## The Impact of the Leadership Journey on Personal and Professional Development

The hike didn't just get us to the mountain's peak; it made us more robust, more resilient, and better prepared for future hikes. Similarly, our leadership journey has shaped us and contributed to our personal and professional development.

Leading a diverse team, promoting inclusive practices, and advocating for gender equality have likely honed your problem-solving skills, deepened your emotional intelligence, and enhanced your ability to drive change. These valuable skills can contribute to your professional development, opening doors to new opportunities and paving the way for career advancement. Recognizing this impact can foster pride and motivate ongoing development.

On a personal level, this journey has likely made you more empathetic, resilient, and self-aware. It may have changed your perspective on diversity and inclusion, broadened your understanding of different experiences, and enriched your values.

Take a moment to reflect on how this journey has impacted your personal and professional development. How has it shaped you as an individual and as a professional?

As we reflect on this journey, let's remember that every step, every stumble, every victory was part of the process. As alchemists, they were the raw materials that we transformed into gold. So, let's take a moment to appreciate the summit's view, celebrate how far we've come, and acknowledge the gold we've discovered along the way.

Because, in the end, the journey is just as valuable as the destination. The challenges, lessons, and growth are the golden nuggets of our leadership journey. So, let's cherish them, learn from them, and use them to navigate the path ahead. After all, the journey of leadership doesn't end at the summit. It's a continuous climb, a never-ending quest for growth, wisdom, and excellence. As we continue this quest, let's remember to appreciate the view, celebrate the victories, and enjoy the journey.

# Key Lessons Learned: The Golden Nuggets

### The Most Important Lessons from the Book

As we pause by our metaphorical campfire, warming our hands on the glowing embers of wisdom we've gathered, let's sift through the ashes and uncover the golden nuggets, the key lessons we've learned from our exploration:

1. **Inclusive Leadership is a Dance, not a Race**: Leading with inclusivity isn't about rushing to the finish line. It's about setting the rhythm, inviting everyone to join in, and celebrating each step we take together. It's about valuing diversity, fostering belonging, and creating a symphony of perspectives that drive innovation and success.
2. **Resilience is Our Superpower**: Our ability to bounce back from setbacks is the secret weapon of every effective leader. It's about viewing challenges as opportunities for growth, embracing change with grace, and navigating uncertainty with courage and adaptability.
3. **Empathy and Emotional Intelligence are Our Guides**: They are our guiding lights in the labyrinth of leadership. They help us understand and connect with our team, navigate conflicts gracefully, and build a culture of respect and understanding.
4. **The Power of Allyship**: Being an ally is like being a lighthouse, guiding those sailing in rough seas. It's about using our privilege to advocate for marginalized people, promote equality, and create a workplace where everyone can thrive.

5. **The Future is Ours to Shape**: As leaders, we are not just participants in the game of change; we are the game-changers. We can shape the future of work, drive innovation, and create a more equitable, inclusive, and just world.

## How These Lessons Apply to Different Leadership Contexts

Now let's think about how these golden nuggets of wisdom can be applied to different leadership contexts:

1. **In a Startup**: Here, building a diverse team from the get-go can foster innovation and drive business growth. Resilience can help navigate the uncertainties of a startup environment, and emotional intelligence can help build a culture where everyone feels valued and heard.
2. **In a Large Corporation**: Implementing inclusive practices can enhance employee engagement, increase retention, and fuel productivity. Allyship can help break down silos, promote cross-department collaboration, and encourage a culture of mutual support and respect.
3. **In a Nonprofit Organization**: Inclusive leadership can ensure that diverse voices are heard, fostering a sense of belonging among staff and volunteers. Empathy and emotional intelligence can enhance relationships with donors, beneficiaries, and the community.
4. **In an Educational Institution**: Fostering resilience can help navigate the challenges of academia, while empathy and emotional intelligence can enhance relationships with students, parents, and faculty. Allyship can promote a culture of equality and respect in the classroom and beyond.

## Strategies for Applying These Lessons in Leadership Practice

Now, let's consider some strategies for applying these lessons to our leadership practice:

1. **Lead with Empathy**: Try to understand your team's experiences and perspectives. Practice active listening, show genuine interest in their ideas, and validate their feelings.

2. **Promote Diversity and Inclusion**: Create an environment that celebrates diversity and makes everyone feel included. Implement inclusive practices, advocate for diversity at all levels, and ensure every voice is heard.

3. **Foster Resilience**: Encourage a growth mindset, promote a learning culture, and view challenges as opportunities for growth. Support your team as they navigate setbacks and celebrate their resilience.

4. **Practice Allyship**: Stand up against discrimination, promote equality, and use your privilege to support those who are marginalized. Be a voice for those who are often overlooked.

5. **Shape the Future**: Take initiative in driving change, encouraging innovation, and leading with vision and purpose. Remember, as a leader, you can shape the future.

As we apply these lessons in our leadership practice, remember that the most beautiful symphonies are not played solo. They require an orchestra of diverse instruments, each playing its unique part, but all in harmony with one another. As leaders, let's strive to conduct our symphony with grace, inclusivity, and resilience, creating a masterpiece of leadership that resonates with harmony and empathy and inspires with its melody.

## Action Steps: Implementing What You've Learned

### Creating a Personal Action Plan

Just as a captain needs a compass to navigate the vast ocean, a leader requires an action plan to steer their leadership development. A personal action plan is your leadership compass, charting your course toward growth and success.

Begin by identifying your leadership goals. Reflect on the challenges you've faced and the areas where you'd like to improve. For instance, you might want to enhance your emotional intelligence, foster a more inclusive culture, or develop resilience.

Next, specify the steps you need to take to achieve these goals. This could include attending workshops, seeking feedback, or implementing new strategies. Each step should be clear, actionable, and aligned with your goals.

Finally, set a timeline for each step. A clear timeframe keeps you on track and enables you to measure your progress.

**Setting Goals for Continued Leadership Growth**

Every incredible journey starts with a destination in mind. In your leadership development journey, your goals are your destinations, guiding you toward growth and success.

When setting your goals, consider your current leadership strengths and areas for improvement. Reflect on the lessons you've picked up from your leadership experiences and how you'd like to grow.

Make your goals **SMART**: Specific, Measurable, Achievable, Relevant, and Time-bound. This ensures your goals are clear, realistic, and aligned with your leadership vision.

Remember to reassess your goals regularly. As you grow as a leader, your goals might evolve, too. Regular reassessments ensure that your goals continue to serve your leadership development needs.

**Strategies for Staying Accountable to Your Action Plan**

Staying accountable to your action plan is like sticking to a fitness routine. It requires commitment, consistency, and a dash of motivation.

One effective strategy is to share your goals and action plan with someone you trust, such as a mentor, colleague, or coach. They can provide support, encouragement, and constructive feedback, keeping you accountable in your leadership journey.

Another strategy is to regularly track your progress. Keep a leadership journal to document your successes, challenges, and learnings. This keeps you accountable and provides valuable insights into your leadership growth.

Finally, celebrate your victories, no matter how small. Each step you take towards your goal is worth celebrating. These celebrations boost your morale and motivate you to stay committed to your action plan.

In the grand scheme of leadership, an action plan is not just a roadmap for development but a commitment to continuous growth and improvement. It's about setting goals, taking consistent steps, and staying accountable to the journey, even when the road gets tough. So, as we navigate the seas of leadership, let's keep our compass handy, our goals in sight, and our spirits high. After all, the adventure has just begun.

## The Ripple Effect: Your Impact as a Leader

### Understanding the Ripple Effect of Leadership

Picture a serene pond. Now, imagine throwing a pebble into it. Note the ripples that emanate from the point of impact, widening and spreading farther, disturbing the tranquility of the waters. This is akin to your impact as a leader - the ripple effect. With each decision you make, each action you take, and each word you utter, you create ripples that extend far beyond your immediate surroundings.

The ripple effect encapsulates the idea that a leader's influence stretches beyond direct interactions. It extends to the team they lead, their organization, and the wider community they serve. Just as a pebble can disturb an entire pond, a leader's actions can impact people and outcomes they may never directly interact with.

### The Impact of Your Leadership on Others

Now, consider the ripples you've created as a leader. Each interaction, each decision, and each word of encouragement or constructive feedback has had an effect. It has shaped perceptions, influenced actions, and affected outcomes. Your leadership style, whether managing conflict or fostering inclusion, has set the tone for your team and shaped their experiences.

The ripples you create can also inspire and motivate others. They can foster a culture of trust, encourage open communication, or promote creativity. They can empower your team members, giving them the confidence to take on new challenges, express their ideas, and reach their full potential.

On a broader scale, your leadership can influence organizational culture, drive business outcomes, and impact societal perceptions and norms. The decisions you make, the practices you implement, and the values you uphold can set a precedent, drive change, and contribute to the broader leadership narrative.

**Strategies for Maximizing Your Leadership Impact**

So, how can you create positive ripples as a leader? How can you maximize your impact and use your influence for good? Here are some strategies to consider:

1. **Lead with Integrity**: Your actions should align with your words. Consistency in your behavior builds trust and sets a positive example for your team.
2. **Promote Open Communication**: Encourage dialogue and ensure everyone feels comfortable sharing their thoughts and ideas. This fosters a culture of transparency and inclusivity.
3. **Encourage Growth**: Provide opportunities for learning and development. Encourage your team members to take on new challenges and to improve continuously.
4. **Recognize and Appreciate**: Acknowledge your team members' efforts and achievements. Show appreciation and give credit where it's due.

5. **Be a Role Model of Inclusivity**: Champion diversity and inclusivity. Foster an environment where everyone feels valued and respected.
6. **Make Decisions Thoughtfully**: Consider the potential impact of your decisions on your team, the organization, and the wider community. Strive for fair, ethical, and beneficial choices in the long run.

As a leader, the ripples you create can have a profound impact. They can shape experiences, influence outcomes, and leave a lasting imprint. So, let's aim to create ripples that inspire, empower, and make a positive difference. Because when we do, we're not just leading; we're also shaping the future, one ripple at a time.

As we close this chapter, pause momentarily and take stock. Reflect on the ripples you've created, the impact you've had, and the leader you've become. Remember, leadership is not just about the destination; it's also about the journey – the growth, the transformation, and the ripples we create along the way. So, as we move forward, let's carry these insights with us, ready to dive deeper and reach wider in our ongoing quest to become the best leaders we can be.

Let's continue to lead with integrity, inspire with our actions, and create positive ripples that reach far and wide. Because in the vast ocean of leadership, we are not just swimmers; we are wave-makers, shaping the tide, steering the current, and charting the course toward a more inclusive, equitable, and impactful future.

## Chapter Summary

"Eureka! Extracting Gold from Chaos: The Alchemy of Women's Leadership" takes us to the summit of our leadership journey, likening it to standing atop a high mountain after facing challenges and transforming chaos into gold. The chapter encourages reflection on personal growth, lessons learned, and the impact of the leadership journey on personal and professional development.

The reflection begins with comparing the initial days of the leadership journey to embarking on a challenging hike, emphasizing the transformation and growth achieved. The narrative then guides the reader to reflect on personal growth, lessons from challenges and successes, and the holistic impact on personal and professional development.

The book's critical lessons are summarized as "golden nuggets," emphasizing the importance of inclusive leadership, resilience, empathy, allyship, and the power to shape the future. These lessons are then applied to various leadership contexts, offering insights into their adaptability in startups, large corporations, nonprofit organizations, and educational institutions.

Strategies for applying these lessons in leadership practice are presented, emphasizing leading with empathy, promoting diversity and inclusion, fostering resilience, practicing allyship, and shaping the future. The chapter concludes with action steps that guide readers in creating a personal action plan, setting goals for continued leadership growth, and staying accountable to their plans.

The ripple effect concept is introduced, illustrating the impact of a leader's actions beyond immediate interactions. The chapter explores the effects of leadership on others, strategies for maximizing leadership impact, and the importance of creating positive ripples through actions aligned with integrity, open communication, growth encouragement, recognition, inclusivity, and thoughtful decision-making.

As the chapter concludes, readers are encouraged to reflect on the ripples they have created as leaders, focusing on shaping experiences, influencing outcomes, and inspiring others. The strategies for maximizing leadership impact are reiterated, emphasizing leaders' profound influence in shaping the future through positive ripples.

The chapter serves as a thoughtful conclusion, prompting readers to appreciate the journey of leadership, cherish the lessons learned, and continue striving to become the best leaders they can be. It highlights the ongoing quest for growth, transformation, and the creation of positive ripples in the vast ocean of leadership.

# CONCLUSION

Well, here we are, my friend, standing at the pinnacle of this literary trek we've embarked on together. We've laughed, pondered, and metaphorically turned lead into gold. You've stuck with me through tales of leadership, through the ups, downs, and roundabouts of the intricate dance of inclusion. You've followed me through the labyrinth of resilience, the symphony of emotional intelligence, and the grand buffet of diversity (where every dish has its unique flavor and adds to the overall feast).

In the immortal words of some brilliant philosopher, "All good things must come to an end." But this signals the start of a new chapter in your leadership journey. As we bid farewell to "The Alchemy of Women's Leadership," consider how you can continue to evolve and influence positive change.

Perhaps you'll continue to hone your leadership skills, transforming the base metals of your workplace into the pure gold of inclusivity. Maybe you'll break down barriers, shattering them like a rock star trashes a hotel room. Or, possibly, you'll inspire the next generation of leaders, passing on wisdom as a beloved grandmother passes on her secret cookie recipe.

Remember, you're not just a speck lost among the stars in this vast universe. You're a supernova, capable of influencing and creating ripples of change that spread far and wide. Your decisions, actions, and words matter-make them count and lead with purpose.

As we close this chapter (quite literally), I want to leave you with a call to action. A call that highlights how your leadership can foster a future where every voice is heard, every contribution is valued, and inclusion is a reality. This is the world we can create, the future we can shape, and it should inspire you to continue making an impact.

So, let's roll up our sleeves, put on our metaphorical alchemist's hat, and get to work. Let's stir the pot of diversity and add a dash of empathy, a sprinkle of resilience, and a dollop of integrity. Let's create a blend as rich and diverse as a potluck dinner at the United Nations. And let's share this feast of inclusivity, not just within our teams or organizations but with the world.

Remember, sustaining your leadership journey requires ongoing effort. Set a personal goal to implement one new inclusive practice each month, and seek out communities or networks that support your growth. You can turn chaos into gold, transform the ordinary into extraordinary, and shape the future of leadership. So, go forth, my friend, and unleash your inner alchemist. Create ripples of change, inspire with your actions, and lead with all the brilliance of a supernova.

So, here's to you, the alchemist, the strategist, the leader. Here's to the journey we've shared, the lessons we've learned, and the future we're about to create. And remember, in the grand buffet of leadership, you're not just a dish; you're the chef, cooking up a storm of change, one leadership meal at a time.

# A QUICK FAVOR

If you enjoyed this book, please consider leaving an honest review where you purchased it. Your feedback helps support the author and independent publishing, and even a sentence or two can make a big difference.

Thank you for reading and supporting independent publishing. Your support means a lot and helps authors continue creating.

# ABOUT KIMBERLY BURK CORDOVA

**Kimberly Burk Cordova** is an author, entrepreneur, and the founder of **Thrive Collective**. This platform supports creators, leaders, and entrepreneurs through publishing, leadership development, and practical tools for real-life growth. With over **30 years of experience** in leadership, technology, and business transformation, she is recognized for transforming big ideas into actionable strategies that deliver results.

Kimberly writes across topics that reflect a life fueled by curiosity: travel and culture, business and leadership, technology and modern work, food and cooking, and the everyday lessons of family life. Her wide-ranging interests invite the audience to see her as relatable and engaging.

Now based in **Santa Fe, New Mexico**, Kimberly finds inspiration in the region's art, culture, and landscapes. She shares life with her husband, Greg, and is a proud mom and grandmother to Vera and Tillman, which adds a personal touch that fosters familiarity and trust.

**Connect & Explore**

- **Thrive Collective** (publishing, leadership, tools): https://www.ThriveCollectiveHQ.com
- **Code Prospector** (audiobook promo codes & reviews): https://www.TheCodeProspector.com

- **Wildflower Artisans** (small-batch silver + genuine stones, curated in Santa Fe): https://wildflowerartisans.com

amazon.com/author/kimberlycordova

goodreads.com/kbcordova

youtube.com/@ThriveCollectiveHQ

facebook.com/ThriveCollectiveHQ

linkedin.com/in/kbcord

tiktok.com/@ThriveCollectiveHQ

instagram.com/thrivecollecthq

pinterest.com/ThriveCollectiveHQ

x.com/ThriveCoHQ

# JOIN OUR MAILING LIST

**Stay Connected with Thrive Collective**

Love history, true crime, leadership insights, and travel guides? Stay in the loop with exclusive updates, behind-the-scenes content, and early access to upcoming releases from Thrive Collective. We value your interest and want you to feel part of our community.

📚 Be the first to hear about new books, special promotions, and subscriber-only content! Your early access makes you a key part of our journey.

✉️ **Join now** and never miss a story, insight, or adventure. Stay connected with interests that matter to you and be part of something bigger.

https://thrivecollectivehq.com/contact

# ALSO BY THRIVE COLLECTIVE

## Shadows of the Past
## Series: by Eliza Hawthorne

- The Vanishing Heiress
- The Music of Murder
- The Silent Witness
- Whispers from the Murder Farm
- Architect of Desire
- The Vanishing Act (Trilogy Collection)

## The Growth Leader Collection:
## by Kimberly Burk Cordova

- The Emotional Intelligence Advantage
- The Leadership Alchemist
- Turning Chaos into Gold
- Leadership Unlocked
- Lead Like You Mean It
- The Procrastination Cure
- Mind Games Exposed

## AI & Automation Blueprint
## Series: by Kimberly Burk Cordova

- Digital Mastery Guide: AI for Productivity
- Digital Mastery Guide: AI Profit Masterclass
- Digital Mastery Guide: Google Ads AI Expertise
- Digital Mastery Guide: Automation in Small Businesses
- Digital Mastery Guide: Business Systemization
- Digital Mastery Guide: AI YouTube Masterclass
- Digital Mastery Guide: Necessary Online Business Tools
- Digital Mastery Guide: Metaverse Explained

## The Profitable Seller Series: by Kimberly Burk Cordova

- FBA Freedom Formula
- Clicks That Convert
- Dropship Mastery

## Profit & Protect: by Kimberly Burk Cordova

- Create It Once, Sell It Forever
- Launch & Leverage
- Udemy Income Mastery

## Empowering Small Businesses Series: by Kimberly Burk Cordova

- The Entrepreneur's Edge
- Artificial Intelligence Unleashed
- Cybersecurity for Entrepreneurs
- Augmented and Virtual Reality

## Campaigns That Convert: by Kimberly Burk Cordova

- The SEO Blueprint
- Affiliate Mastery Blueprint

## Travel Series: by Kimberly Burk Cordova

- Santa Fe Uncovered
- Santa Fe
- Denver Dossier
- Portland Your Way
- Stress Relief Travel Coloring Book For Adults

## Eat Without Fear Series: by Kimberly Burk Cordova

- Eat Light, Live Bright: Low-Fat Recipes & Meal Plans

## Kitchen-Table Guide from a Tech Oma: by Kimberly Burk Cordova

- Kids + AI

## Content Strategy Ladder: by Kimberly Burk Cordova

- Audience X-Ray Vision

## Young Legends: Inspiring True Stories of Kids' Favorite Athletes, Leaders, and Inventors

- Basketball Legends for Kids
- Soccer Legends for Kids
- Game Changers: Women Athletes
- Baseball Legends You Should Know
- The Caveman's Guide to Mental Toughness for Young Athletes

## Journal Series: by Cordova Creations

- Align & Shine
- The 369 Method Manifestation
- Disconnect To Reconnect
- Simplify Your Life
- Just Write
- I Am Too Old for This Sh*t
- Dear Mom and Dad
- My Cat Rocks
- My Dog Rocks

- My Soft Girl Rocks
- My Inner Badass Rocks
- My Son Rocks
- My Daughter Rocks
- My Husband Rocks
- My Wife Rocks

# REFERENCES

- *50 Women Who Made American Political History* https://time.com/4551817/50-women-political-history-2/
- *The Top 10 Influential Women in Leadership for 2023* https://www.nsls.org/blog/the-top-10-influential-women-in-leadership-for-2023
- *Female Leadership: Overcoming Stereotypes About ...* https://www.forbes.com/sites/forbescoachescouncil/2021/01/26/female-leadership-overcoming-stereotypes-about-choosing-the-best-leader/
- *10 Most Common Leadership Styles and Their Pros ...* https://www.themuse.com/advice/common-leadership-styles-with-pros-and-cons
- *Data on Women Leaders in the U.S.* https://www.pewresearch.org/social-trends/fact-sheet/the-data-on-women-leaders/
- *Women and the Labyrinth of Leadership* https://hbr.org/2007/09/women-and-the-labyrinth-of-leadership
- *KPMG study finds 75% of executive women experience ...* https://info.kpmg.us/news-perspectives/people-culture/kpmg-study-finds-most-female-executives-experience-imposter-syndrome.html
- *Recognizing and Responding to Microaggressions at Work* https://hbr.org/2022/05/recognizing-and-responding-to-microaggressions-at-work
- *Intersectionality and Leadership* https://www.regent.edu/acad/global/publications/ijls/new/vol3iss2/IJLS_V3Is2_Richardson_Loubier.pdf
- *Why Diverse Teams Are Smarter* https://hbr.org/2016/11/why-diverse-teams-are-smarter
- *Anti-Racist Leadership: Why It Matters and How to Become ...* https://embracingequity.org/blog/2021/8/19/anti-racist-leadership-why-it-matters-and-how-to-become-one
- *The Key to Inclusive Leadership* https://hbr.org/2020/03/the-key-to-inclusive-leadership
- *Emotional Intelligence in Leadership: Why It's Important* https://online.hbs.edu/blog/post/emotional-intelligence-in-leadership
- *Inclusive and Empathic Leadership: Strategies for Success* https://blog.aebetancourt.com/inclusive-empathic-leadership
- *5 Effective Strategies for Having Difficult Conversations at ...* https://www.td.org/atd-blog/5-effective-strategies-for-having-difficult-conversations-at-work
- *The Role of Emotional Intelligence in Conflict Resolution* https://www.linkedin.com/pulse/role-emotional-intelligence-conflict-resolution-how-manage-gaur

# References

- *Adapting Leadership Styles to Reflect Generational ...* https://www.ncbi.nlm.nih.gov/pmc/articles/PMC6116874/
- *How Decision-Making Changes With Age* https://www.simonsfoundation.org/2022/03/02/how-decision-making-changes-with-age
- *Bridging Generational Divides in Your Workplace* https://hbr.org/2023/01/bridging-generational-divides-in-your-workplace
- *Harnessing the Power of Age Diversity* https://hbr.org/2022/03/harnessing-the-power-of-age-diversity
- *Crafting an Impactful Leadership Philosophy: Guide & Examples* https://northwest.education/insights/careers/what-is-leadership-philosophy/#:~:text=Inspiration%20and%20motivation%3A%20Leaders%20with,to%20work%20towards%20common%20goals.
- *Exploring Leadership Styles - When East Meets West - BRIDGE* https://bridge-partnership.com/leadership-styles-when-east-meets-west/
- *From transactional to transformational leadership: Learning ...* https://www.sciencedirect.com/science/article/pii/009026169090061S
- *The Importance of Ethical Leadership and Moral Courage ...* https://icma.org/articles/pm-magazine/importance-ethical-leadership-and-moral-courage-public-management
- *5 Stories from Trailblazing Women Leaders* https://www.inc.com/partners-in-leadership/5-stories-from-high-impact-women-leaders.html
- *Leaders' role in building resilience and psychologically ...* https://www.ncbi.nlm.nih.gov/pmc/articles/PMC9127620/
- *Seven Self-Care Strategies Of Successful Leaders* https://www.forbes.com/sites/forbescoachescouncil/2020/02/21/seven-self-care-strategies-of-successful-leaders/
- *7 Strategies to Build a More Resilient Team* https://hbr.org/2021/01/7-strategies-to-build-a-more-resilient-team
- *The importance of psychological safety in the workplace* https://www.mckinsey.com/featured-insights/leadership/five-fifty-is-it-safe
- *Unlocking Effective Allyship: 5 Key Strategies for Lasting ...* https://www.linkedin.com/pulse/unlocking-effective-allyship-5-key-strategies-lasting-change-pqhie?trk=article-ssr-frontend-pulse_more-articles_related-content-card
- *The Key to Inclusive Leadership* https://hbr.org/2020/03/the-key-to-inclusive-leadership
- *Case Studies: Embed Inclusion Into the Organization's Culture* https://hr.mcleanco.com/research/case-studies-embed-inclusion-into-the-organization-s-culture
- *Role of female leadership in corporate innovation* https://www.emerald.com/insight/content/doi/10.1108/GM-01-2022-0028/full/pdf?title=role-of-female-leadership-in-corporate-innovation-a-systematic-literature-review
- *Women's Leadership and Participation: Case studies on ...* https://policy-practice.

oxfam.org/resources/womens-leadership-and-participation-case-studies-on-learning-for-action-115530/

- *The Role of Mentorship in Women's Leadership ...* https://elvtr.com/blog/the-role-of-mentorship-in-womens-leadership-development-why-mentors-matter
- *Women in Leadership Trends* https://globalwellnessinstitute.org/women-in-leadership-trends/
- *Experiences and outcomes of a women's leadership ...* https://journalofleadershiped.org/jole_articles/experiences-and-outcomes-of-a-womens-leadership-development-program-a-phenomenological-investigation/
- *The Key to Inclusive Leadership* https://hbr.org/2020/03/the-key-to-inclusive-leadership
- *Women in Leadership: 5 Strategies for Advancing Your ...* https://www.linkedin.com/pulse/women-leadership-5-strategies-advancing-your-career-kate-hutson
- *The Business Case For Women In Leadership* https://www.forbes.com/sites/tomaspremuzic/2022/03/02/the-business-case-for-women-in-leadership/

www.ingramcontent.com/pod-product-compliance
Lightning Source LLC
Chambersburg PA
CBHW070918290526
45795CB00001B/348